A NEW OWNER'S
GUIDE TO
SIBERIAN HUSKIES

JG-127

The Publisher wishes to acknowledge the following owners of the dogs in this book: Franca Burini, Phyllis Carlson, Jean Edwards, Ann Gourman, Beverly Johnson, Kathleen, Norbert and Trish Kanzler, Earl Kavas, Monville-Kisteman, Marelyn Peterson, Kathy Povey, Marcelino Pozo, Richard Stacks, Ceasar Vassallo.

Photographers: John Ashbey, Franca Burini, Phyllis Carlson, Jean C. Edwards, Isabelle Francais, Ann Gourman, Beverly Johnson, Kathleen Kanzler, Norbert Kanzler, Earl Kavas, Monville-Kisteman, Robert Pearcy, Marelyn Peterson, Kathy Povey, Marcelino Pozo, Richard Stacks, Sumner, Chuck & Sandy Tatham, Karen Taylor, Ceasar Vassallo, Dr. Wachberger.

The author acknowledges the contribution of Judy Iby for the following chapters: Sport of Purebred Dogs, Health Care for Your Dog, Traveling with Your Dog, and Behavior and Canine Communication.

Dedication: This book is dedicated to the most special breed in the world, the Siberian Husky. All of my dogs have a special place in my heart. To Champion Innisfree's Lobo, my first home-bred champion. Also to Thor, Pegasus, Sierra Cinnar, my special friend Rannic, Roadster and Ice-T. All champions, all special friends in my life, each unique in their own way. "It hurts so much when you leave."

Distributed in the UNITED STATES to the Pet Trade by T.F.H. Publications, Inc., One T.F.H. Plaza, Neptune City, NJ 07753; distributed in the UNITED STATES to the Bookstore and Library Trade by National Book Network, Inc. 4720 Boston Way, Lanham MD 20706; in CANADA to the Pet Trade by H & L Pet Supplies Inc., 27 Kingston Crescent, Kitchener, Ontario N2B 2T6; Rolf C. Hagen Inc., 3225 Sartelon St. Laurent-Montreal Quebec H4R 1E8; in CANADA to the Book Trade by Vanwell Publishing Ltd., 1 Northrup Crescent, St. Catharines, Ontario L2M 6P5 ; in ENGLAND by T.F.H. Publications, PO Box 15, Waterlooville PO7 6BQ; in AUSTRALIA AND THE SOUTH PACIFIC by T.F.H. (Australia), Pty. Ltd., Box 149, Brookvale 2100 N.S.W., Australia; in NEW ZEALAND by Brooklands Aquarium Ltd. 5 McGiven Drive, New Plymouth, RD1 New Zealand; in Japan by T.F.H. Publications, Japan—Jiro Tsuda, 10-12-3 Ohjidai, Sakura, Chiba 285, Japan; in SOUTH AFRICA by Lopis (Pty) Ltd., P.O. Box 39127, Booysens, 2016, Johannesburg, South Africa. Published by T.F.H. Publications, Inc.
MANUFACTURED IN THE
UNITED STATES OF AMERICA
BY T.F.H. PUBLICATIONS, INC.

A NEW OWNER'S GUIDE TO
SIBERIAN HUSKIES

KATHLEEN KANZLER

Contents

The Siberian Husky's expression is keen, friendly, and even mischievous.

Siberian Huskies are still pulling sleds in races and for sheer enjoyment around the world.

Husky puppies like these playful littermates are naturally irresistible.

With a nutritious diet, Huskies grow to be all-around athletes.

The dignified Siberian Husky is a loyal but free-spirited breed.

PREFACE

The purpose of this book is to introduce the Siberian Husky, body and soul, to my readers. Of all the dogs in the world, the Siberian Husky was certainly most favored when nature created him. A beautiful, dense coat, the body of a superb athlete, an exquisite head and expressive eyes—all the indomitable spirit of this playful, sometimes mischievous companion and friend. The only true love that money can buy. The Siberian is a wonderful friend, family companion in all activities, and even a working member of the family.

This book is a how-to book. How to raise this unique, special dog with most of his unusual instincts to survive in a hostile Arctic world intact. He did survive in this world because he could adapt. He could be a companion to man and a playmate for their children. He could be a diligent worker on the sled with incredible determination and endurance. His exploits in the service of man in the Siberian Arctic, the Alaskan wilderness and the Canadian far north in hunting, rescue work and in transportation and carrying supplies have given him a hero status that is unsurpassed today.

This book is my opportunity to share with you, the reader, my life-long knowledge of this wonderful breed. The Siberian Husky's love of life and free spirit require a special owner—one who will appreciate a partnership with a dog, not an owner who demands a master/slave relationship. Siberians are extremely smart, willing-to-please dogs, but they want to be a part of it, not just be told what to do. To be a successful owner of a Siberian, you must respect this special relationship with your dog. Do not let his free spirit and love of life go undisciplined. He must adapt to the world in which you live. I want every Siberian to have a great life with caring owners. The Siberian must be trained to achieve this greatness. My goal in writing this book is to present a true picture of the needs of the Siberian Husky so that he can achieve the title of "Splendid Companion."

Kathleen Kanzler
94 Ryan Road
Chateaugay, NY 12920

ACKNOWLEDGMENTS

To the INNISFREE FAMILY all over the world, I wish to express my thanks for their encouragement and advice in this great adventure. Innisfree is not just my immediate family. It includes all of my friends and acquaintances all over the world. My good friends in Japan, Germany, Belgium, Austria, Italy, Spain, South Africa, Australia, Argentina, Brazil, Mexico, Israel, and all the other countries throughout Europe, Asia, South America, Canada and, of course, the United States who have made this wonderful experience possible. To each of them I owe a special thanks. To all of the photographers, both professional and amateur, who contributed to the book. I hope you enjoy seeing your photos in print. And of course, to my family: husband Norbert, daughters Patricia and Sheila, son John, daughter-in-law Pam, and son-in-law Frank Napoli—all deserve a special thanks.

No list of acknowledgments would be complete without a mention of some of the greats in the dog world who directly affected my life. The list of mentors in my learning about dogs in general and Siberians in particular is very close to my heart. Erma Ransom of Collie fame in the 1940s; Julia Gasow, also of Detroit, Michigan; Marie Slattery, Miniature Schnauzers, a great teacher and friend; Thelma and Curtis Brown, whose help allowed me to expand on my knowledge of structure and how it affects movement; Lorna Demidoff, a great lady, a role model of how to conduct oneself in the world of dogs, a warm gracious person and a true lover of the Siberian Husky; Doc Lombard, a champion dog driver and a wonderful man; Leonard Seppala, the catalyst who brought together the great fraternity of the Siberian Husky; Charlie and Carolyn Posey of Yeso Pac Siberian fame; a special admiration and fondness for Marlytuck's Peggy Grant; Frosty Aire's Donna Foster; and Alakasan's Peggy Koehler; as well as all the other wonderful people in the special world of purebred dogs. The list of people who have influenced my life with the Siberian Husky is worldwide and to all who have helped me, I give a special thank you.

HISTORY of the Siberian Husky

The Siberian Husky was recognized as a pure breed by the American Kennel Club (AKC) in 1930. The first breed standard was published in the April 1932 issue of the *Pure Bred Dogs/ American Kennel Gazette* magazine. Many of the first Siberian Huskies to be registered with the American Kennel Club were from Julian Hurley's Northern Lights Kennel in Fairbanks, Alaska. The first Siberian Husky to become an AKC champion was Northern Lights Kobuck. Since this time, the Husky has continued to be successful in the show ring and has enjoyed a steady rise in popularity. In 1995, the AKC *Gazette* listed the Siberian Husky as the 18th most popular breed, based on the number of individual dogs registered.

The arrival of the Siberian Husky in America can most directly be traced to the Alaskan gold rush. The gold rush, which occurred at the turn of the century, created an unprecedented need for a great number of sled dog teams in Alaska as a means of transportation. Dogs were pressed into service from all parts of the United States and Canada. Some of them were ill-suited for working in the harsh Arctic environment. For centuries, man has used animals for sport, and the gold rush era was no exception. Local races were

organized between dog teams and, in 1908, the first All-Alaska Sweepstakes race was held. This race, from Nome to Candle and back, covered a distance

It was during the Alaskan gold rush that Siberian Huskies became popular as hardy sled dogs.

Hurley's team of ten Siberian Huskies in Fairbanks, Alaska. The lead dog's name is Jack Frost.

of 408 miles and the purse was $10,000. A Russian fur trader by the name of "Goosak" had imported a team of Arctic dogs from Siberia and placed third in this race. This created an interest in importing this type of dog, and Fox Maule Ramsey, a son of the Earl of Dalhousie, imported 70 dogs from the Anadyr River region.

The All-Alaska Sweepstakes were run from 1908 until 1917, when they were interrupted by World War I. The races for 1915, 1916, and 1917 were won by Leonard Seppala and his team of Siberian sled dogs. This established a racing fame for Seppala that continued into the 1920s and 1930s in the New England area and resulted in sled dog racing becoming a demonstration event in the New England area. Sled dog racing was also a demonstration event in the 1932 winter Olympic games in Lake Placid, New York.

An outbreak of diphtheria in Nome, Alaska in 1925 was the event that sparked the popularity of the Arctic sled dog, particularly the Siberian Husky. Air transportation was in its infancy and the 80-mile-per-hour winds and blizzard conditions prevented the transportation of anti-toxin from Anchorage to Nome by air. The Alaska railroad could transport the anti-toxin to Nenana (a distance of 297 miles), but it would have to be sent the remaining 658 miles by relays of dog teams. Dog teams and drivers were organized and the race to save Nome was on. Progress reports were sent by telegraph as the anti-toxin was transferred from driver to driver. Gunnar Kasan, the last relay driver, reached Nome at 5:30 p.m. on February 2, delivering the anti-toxin in time to prevent further spread of the disease. The trip from Nenana to Nome took just five and a half days. This was a remarkable event considering that the US mail teams normally took 25 days to cover this same distance. The person to drive the longest leg of the relay was Leonard Seppala. Seppala drove a distance of 340 miles, while the longest distance for any other relay driver was 53 miles. Both Kasan and Seppala drove teams of Siberian Huskies.

After the serum race, Seppala toured the United States giving demonstrations of Arctic life and Siberian Husky sled dogs. The remarkable performances of these Siberian Huskies gave them a place in history and started them on their way to the popularity that is enjoyed by their offspring today.

The origin of the modern-day Siberian Husky has been traced to the Chukchi peoples of eastern Siberia through the import of sled dogs to Nome and, later, directly to New England. Unfortunately, it is difficult to trace the history of the

A modern-day racer, this is Marcelino Pozo with his Husky team in Sierra Nevada, Spain!

breed because in the 1930s the Soviet policy was to discredit the various native breeds and to develop a standardized division of the Northern dogs into four basic types: the sled dog, the reindeer herding dog, and two types of hunting dog (large game and small game). These dogs are termed "Laikas," and the sled dogs used by the Chukchi were discouraged by the Soviet regime. Thus, the Siberian Husky as we know it today, although developed from dogs imported from eastern Siberia, is considered an American breed; the American Kennel Club publishes the official standard used throughout the world.

With snow covering his nose, it looks like Innisfree Nanook is at home in the Austrian Alps.

Commander Robert Peary drives sled teams across the Arctic on his march to the North Pole.

EARLY KENNELS IN NEW ENGLAND

Following the Nenana to Nome serum relay, Leonard Seppala toured the United States with 43 dogs, most of them Siberian Huskies, and gave demonstrations on sled dogs and Arctic life. When his contract for exhibits came to an end in January of 1927, Seppala left his last show, which was at Madison Square Garden in New York City, to stay in Wonalancet, New Hampshire, at the kennels of Arthur Walden. While in New England, Seppala's performance at races with Siberian Huskies established the Siberian as a race dog. While racing in Poland Springs, Maine, Seppala met Mrs. Ricker and later started a kennel at her hotel in Poland Springs. This kennel, the Seppala/Ricker Kennel, lasted from 1927 to 1932 and established the Siberian Husky in the East. Seppala's famous lead dog, "Togo," lived out his last days with Mrs. Ricker and was popularized in children's books around this time.

Today, Siberian Huskies are popular around the world. This is Toru Oki, a famous Japanese singer, with his five dogs.

A pioneer of the breed in the US, this is Lorna Demidoff with a team of Huskies at her home in Fitzwilliam, New Hampshire.

Two other kennels, Chinook and Monadnock, were instrumental in getting the Siberian Husky recognized by the American Kennel Club. Eva "Short" Seeley and her husband Milton assisted in training sled dogs for Admiral Byrd's expedition to the South Pole and operated Arthur Walden's Chinook kennels while Walden accompanied Admiral Byrd on his journey. On Walden's return, he sold the kennel to the Seeleys. Sled dogs were trained here for the second and third Byrd expeditions as well as for use by the US Army during World War II.

The second kennel, Monadnock, that of Lorna Demidoff, was located in Fitzwilliam, New Hampshire, and operated from the 1930s until the mid 1970s. These kennels provided much of the foundation stock behind the Siberian Huskies of today and were instrumental in getting AKC recognition for the breed. The beautiful sled dogs developed by these kennels live on in the Huskies of today—in the show ring, on the sled trails, and in the home as family pets.

CHARACTERISTICS of the Siberian Husky

There are few people who are not impressed at their first sight of a Siberian Husky. If any breed has the capability of stopping a crowd with its beautiful eyes alone, it is this one. Adaptable, cheerful and loyal, this medium-sized, ancient Nordic breed is well suited to both country and city life and continues to find new admirers wherever he goes. With proper attention and care, this double-coated breed is suited to all kinds of temperatures and environments, from cold weather and deep snow to hot, humid summer days. In every case, protection from extreme temperatures is ensured by the Husky's well-insulated coat.

The history of the Siberian Husky fascinates all dog lovers. Believed to trace back thousands of years to Asian migrants who harnessed and befriended Arctic-wolf crosses, the Siberian Husky, working in packs of six or more, pulled sleds for the Eskimos and assisted these nomads in a variety of hunting and working tasks. Although this multi-talented dog was originally bred principally as a sled dog, it currently performs many other roles in modern society. Besides being a wonderful family pet, he also serves as an active companion in a variety of outdoor sports and activities. Siberians are great jogging partners, willing to run as far as you can. Remember to use the same conditioning routine for your dog as you use for yourself. While the Husky can run great distances on an Arctic tundra, he shouldn't be over stressed running on paved roads, especially in hot, humid weather.

Siberian Huskies are adaptable, cheerful and loyal, and they love to participate in family functions.

Siberians are by nature active dogs and from puppyhood on need acceptable outlets for their energy. These two pass the time playing with safe toys.

In summer, many owners enjoy outdoor activities such as hiking in the woods, backpacking and camping with their Siberian. Huskies are handy because they can carry their own backpack. Likewise, children love the Husky because he is tolerant and often affectionate. The list of the Siberian's hobbies are nearly as long as his talents; agility trials, tracking, racing, and skijoring are just some of the Husky's favorites.

Because the Siberian can be an energetic, active breed with an independent attitude and mind, he is not suited for everyone. The Siberian's strong will and independent nature endear him with involved, experienced dog owners. Most breeders do not recommend the Siberian for the first-time dog owner, as the dog may be too challenging for the neophyte. If you've had success with other breeds of dog, the Siberian may be your best choice for a new pet.

The Siberian makes an ideal family dog. His cheerful, fun-loving nature makes him a great asset to any active family. Siberians are not guard dogs; however, their value as a protector is only a deterrent to intruders who might hear the dog's primitive and intense bark.When properly trained, the Siberian should be trustworthy with all the members of the family, as the breed has long been hailed as a friend of children and elderly people alike.

STANDARD for the Siberian Husky

T he standard of any breed is the written description of that breed. The standard for the Siberian Husky is the "blueprint" by which individual dogs are compared to the ideal specimen. The Siberian standard is not a restrictive one. It applies sound principles of proper structure and correct movement into the requirement for a good Siberian Husky. The Siberian Husky Club of America is responsible for developing and approving the standard. This standard does not emphasize cosmetic traits. Any color or combination of colors, and any eye color or combination of eye colors is allowed, with no preference given to any color or combination of colors. The only disqualification is for dogs that exeed 23 ½ inches at the shoulder or bitches that exceed 22 inches at the shoulder. The Siberian is a medium-sized working dog, and the standard emphasizes that point. (Italics are author's comments on the standard.)

This is American and Canadian Champion Innisfree Fire and Frost, CGC, winning Best of Breed at the prestigious Westminster Kennel Club show in 1993.

OFFICIAL AKC STANDARD FOR THE SIBERIAN HUSKY:

General Appearance—The Siberian Husky is a medium-size working dog, quick and light on his feet and free and graceful in action. His moderately compact and well-furred body, erect ears and brush tail suggest his Northern heritage. His characteristic gait is smooth and seemingly effortless. He performs his original function in harness most capably, carrying a light load at a moderate speed

At conformation shows, dogs are judged against the standards for their breeds.

The standard describes the Husky as a well-balanced, athletic animal. Ch. Innisfree's Irish Derby fits the bill for this judge in Philadelphia.

over great distances. His body proportions and form reflect this basic balance of power, speed and endurance. The males of the Siberian Husky breed are masculine but never coarse; the bitches are feminine but without weakness of structure. In proper condition, with muscle firm and well developed, the Siberian Husky does not carry excess weight.

The Siberian Husky is a medium-sized working dog, appearing neither heavy and coarse, nor fine and weak. A well-balanced, athletic animal is desired.

Size, Proportion, Substance—Height—Dogs, 21 to 23 inches at the withers. Bitches 20 to 22 inches at the withers. Weight—Dogs, 45 to 60 pounds. Bitches 35 to 50 pounds. Weight is in proportion to height. The measurements mentioned above represent the extreme height and weight limits with no preference given to either extreme. Any appearance of excessive bone or weight should be penalized. In profile, the length of the body from the point of the shoulder to the rear point of the croup is slightly longer than the height of the body from the ground to the top of the withers. **Disqualifications**—Dogs over 23 inches and bitches over 22 inches.

It is important to remember that a range of size is permitted in the Siberian Husky. No preference should be given to those near the top or bottom of the standard. Both are correct. Over size is a disqualification. If the judge questions the size, the animal should be measured with an official AKC wicket.

Head—*Expression* is keen, but friendly, interested and even mischievous. *Eyes* almond-shaped, moderately spaced and set a trifle obliquely. Eyes may be brown or blue in color; one of each or parti-colored are acceptable. **Faults**—eyes set too obliquely; set too close together. *Ears* of medium size, triangular in shape, close fitting and set high on the head. They are thick, well furred, and slightly arched at the back and strongly erect, with slightly rounded tips pointing straight up. *Faults*—Ears too large in proportion to the head; too wide set; not strongly erect. *Skull* of medium size and in proportion to the body; slightly rounded on top and tapering from the widest point of the eyes. *Faults*—Head clumsy or heavy; head too finely chiseled. *Stop*—The stop is well-defined and the bridge of the nose is straight from the stop to the tip. *Fault*—

This dog has the keen expression and almond-shaped eyes characteristic of the Husky.

Insufficient stop. *Muzzle* of medium length; that is, the distance from the tip of the nose to the stop is equal to the distance from the stop to the occiput. The muzzle is of

19

medium width, tapering gradually to the nose, with the tip neither pointed nor square. *Faults*—Muzzle either too snipy or too coarse; muzzle too short or too long. *Nose* black in gray, tan or black dogs; liver in copper dogs; may be flesh-colored in copper dogs; may be flesh-colored in pure-white dogs. The pink-streaked "snow nose" is acceptable. Lips are well pigmented and close fitting. *Teeth* closing in a scissors bite. *Fault*—Any bite other than scissors.

Neck, Topline, Body—*Neck* medium in length, arched and carried proudly erect when dog is standing. When moving at a trot, the neck is extended so that the head is carried slightly forward. *Faults*—Neck too short and thick; neck too long. *Chest* deep and strong, but not too broad, with the deepest point being just behind and level with the elbows. The ribs are well sprung from the spine but flattened on the sides to allow for freedom of action. *Faults*—Chest too broad; "barrel ribs"; ribs too flat or weak. *Back*—The back is straight and strong, with a level topline from withers to croup. It is of medium length, neither cobby nor slack from excessive length. The loin is taut and lean,

The Husky standard describes the neck, topline and body of a dog designed to pull sleds long distances.

You can see the deep chest and prominent sternum on Brazilian International Champion Innisfree's Priority One, shown here winning Best in Show in Brazil.

narrower than the rib cage, and with a slight tuck-up. The croup slopes away from the spine at an angle, but never so steeply as to restrict the rearward thrust of the hind legs. **Faults**—Weak or slack back; roached back; sloping topline.

Many of the muscles controlling the front are connected through the neck. A correct neck is necessary for proper movement. A medium-length and well-arched neck provides for maximum endurance. The neck should not join the topline as is the case with a straight-shouldered dog. If the shoulder is too steep, the dog is forced to move with the head and neck more erect, thus causing an up-and-down movement which is very inefficient. Where endurance is required, a deep chest is very important since it contains the heart and lungs. A broad chest would impede the follow-through of the front legs. The desired chest is deep, with ribs well sprung but flat on the sides. A prominent sternum bone is desired.

Tail—The well furred tail of fox brush shape is set on just below the level of the topline, and is usually carried over the back in a graceful sickle curve when the dog is at attention. When carried up, the tail does not curl to either side of the body, nor does it snap flat against the back. A trailing tail is normal for the dog when in repose. Hair on the tail is of medium length and approximately the same length on the tip, sides and bottom, giving the appearance of a round brush. *Faults*—A snapped or tightly curled tail; highly plumed tail; tail set too low or too high.

The set of the tail is dependent on the angle of the croup. A slightly sloping croup places the base of the tail just below the level of the topline. The tail carriage changes depending on whether the dog is moving, in repose or if he is excited. A snap or tightly curled tail is faulted.

Forequarters—**Shoulders**—the shoulder blade is well laid back. The upper arm angles slightly backward from point of shoulder to elbow, and is never perpendicular to the ground. The muscles and ligaments holding the shoulder to the rib cage are firm and well developed. *Faults*—Straight shoulders; loose shoulders. **Forelegs**—When standing and viewed from the front, the legs are moderately spaced, parallel and straight, with the elbows close to the body and turned neither in nor out. Viewed from the side, pasterns are slightly slanted, with the pastern joint strong, but flexible. Bone is substantial but never heavy. Length of leg from elbow to ground is slightly more than the distance from the elbow to the top of withers. Dewclaws on forelegs may be removed. *Faults*—Weak pasterns; too heavy bone; too narrow or too wide in the front;

This dog's tail illustrates the well-furred fox brush shape that is correct for the Siberian Husky.

out at the elbows. *Feet* oval in
shape but not long. The paws
are medium in size, compact
and well furred between the
toes and pads. The pads are
tough and thickly cushioned.
The paws neither turn in nor
out when the dog is in natural
stance. *Faults*—Soft or splayed
toes; paws too large and
clumsy; paws too small and
delicate; toeing in or out.
Ideal shoulder lay back
would approach 45 degrees.
This allows maximum reach
and follow-through. The
request for muscles to be firm
and well developed is in the
interest of endurance and

*Although this dog isn't in a
classic show pose, you can see
his oval feet, powerful thighs
and well-defined hock joint.*

proper movement. Length of leg should be slightly longer than
the depth of the body. This is in the interest of optimal speed
and endurance.

Hindquarters—When standing and viewed from the rear,
the hind legs are moderately spaced and parallel. The upper
thighs are well muscled and powerful, the stifles well bent, the
hock joint well-defined and set low to the ground. Dewclaws,
if any, are to be removed. *Faults*—Straight stifles, cowhocks,
too narrow or too wide in the rear.

The hindquarters of a dog generate under-thrust and power.
A low-set hock joint requires less muscular activity and is more
enduring. The actual stiffle bend is produced by the angle at
which the upper and lower thigh bones meet and will vary
according to the relative length of these bones.

Coat—The coat of the Siberian Husky is double and medium
in length, giving a well furred appearance, but is never so long
as to obscure the clean-cut outline of the dog. The undercoat is
soft and dense and of sufficient length to support the outer
coat. The guard hairs of the outer coat are straight and
somewhat smooth lying, never harsh nor standing straight off
from the body. It should be noted that the absence of the
undercoat during the shedding season is normal. Trimming of

whiskers and fur between the toes and around the feet to present a neater appearance is permissible. Trimming the fur on any other part of the dog is not to be condoned and should be severely penalized. *Faults*—Long, rough, or shaggy coat; texture too harsh or too silky; trimming of the coat, except as permitted above.

Color—All colors from black to pure white are allowed. A variety of markings on the head is common, including many striking patterns not found in other breeds.

The one blue and one brown eyes on this Siberian are acceptable in the standard, as is the pink streak in the nose (called a "snow nose"). All give this handsome fellow a striking appearance.

The Siberian coat is unique among Arctic breeds because of the medium length. There exists a range of coat lengths from about one inch to three inches, but all coats should have an outer coat and a dense undercoat except when the dog is shedding. A trimmed or scissored coat should be severely faulted. It should be noted that all colors are permitted with no preference given to any color.

Gait—The Siberian Husky's characteristic gait is smooth and seemingly effortless. He is quick and light on his feet, and when in the show ring should be gaited on a loose lead at a moderately fast trot, exhibiting good reach in the forequarters and good drive in the hindquarters. When viewed from the front to rear while moving at a walk the Siberian Husky does not single-track, but as the speed increases the legs gradually angle inward until the pads are falling on a line directly under the longitudinal center of the body. As the pad marks converge, the forelegs and hind legs are carried straight forward, with neither elbows nor stifles turned in or out. Each

Any color is allowed in the Siberian, including striking patterns like the black and brown patches on this dog.

Brendan and Kristen Johnson trust their dogs Kimmy and Keela to pull their stagecoach. Good disposition is one of the Husky's most important characteristics.

hind leg moves in the path of the foreleg on the same side. When the dog is gaiting, the topline remains firm and level. **Faults**—Short, prancing or choppy gait, lumbering or rolling gait; crossing or crabbing.

Balance is the key to movement. The request for single tracking and for the rear legs to follow in the line of the front is in the interest of efficiency. A dog who is more angulated in the rear than in the front is likely to crab. Short, prancing or choppy gaits are usually caused by insufficient front angulation or straight pasterns. This will cause the dog to bob up and down rather than move in the line of travel. He will be slower and tire more quickly. When moving, the Siberian should appear light and quick on his feet and exhibit a smooth and effortless gait. The Siberian should be evaluated closely from the side. Smooth, easy side movement exhibiting ground covering ability is the Siberian's specialty.

Temperament—The characteristic temperament of the Siberian Husky is friendly and gentle, but also alert and outgoing. He does not display the possessive qualities of the guard dog, nor is he overly suspicious of strangers or aggressive with other dogs. Some measure of reserve and dignity may be expected in the mature dog. His intelligence, tractability, and eager disposition make him an agreeable companion and willing worker.

Temperament is of utmost importance in a Siberian Husky. An aggressive dog is not a team dog and since the Siberian is a sled dog, any sign of aggression toward other dogs should be severely penalized.

Innisfree Firedance is a registered therapy dog, a job the well-bred Husky is particularly suited to.

Summary—The most important breed characteristics of the Siberian Husky are medium size, moderate bone, well balanced proportions, ease and freedom of movement, proper coat, pleasing head and ears, correct tail and good disposition. Any appearance of excessive bone or weight, constricted or clumsy gait, or long, rough coat should be penalized. The Siberian Husky never appears so heavy or coarse as to suggest a frightening animal; nor is he so light and fragile as to suggest a sprint-racing animal. In both sexes the Siberian Husky gives the appearance of being capable of great endurance. In addition to the faults already noted, the obvious structural faults common to all breeds are as undesirable in the Siberian Husky as in any other breed, even though they are not specifically mentioned herein.

DISQUALIFICATION - *Dogs over 23 inches and bitches over 22 inches.*

SELECTING Your Siberian Husky

A s a prospective owner of a Siberian Husky, it is up to you to use sensible care in finding a well-bred, healthy, good-tempered dog for you and your family. How to do this properly is the focus of this section. First, find a good breeder of Siberian Huskies. Call the American Kennel Club in New York City for a list of breeders. The AKC should also give you a phone number for a breeder referral representative of the Siberian Husky Club of America who can give you names of members who breed Huskies in your area. Other places to look are monthly dog magazines that advertise breeders and the latest information system, the Internet.

If possible, you can always attend an AKC-sponsored show or match. You will learn something about Siberians from everyone you speak to. You will soon learn, perhaps to your surprise, that serious breeders care very little about coat color and eye color in their dogs. The standard for the breed is very specific in that all coat colors and eye colors are allowed with no preference given to any particular one. The main focus of their breeding programs is to produce a sound dog, both physically and mentally, that is as close to the standard as possible.

ABOUT BREEDERS

There are certain things that good breeders do to ensure healthy puppies. The sire (father) and dam (mother) of the puppies you are considering for purchase should have their hips X-rayed and their eyes checked by a canine ophthalmologist. The breeder of the puppies should be knowledgeable about the breed and the puppies they have for sale. He should be helpful and informative over the phone. Good breeders will interview prospective buyers. They will want to know where the dog will live during the day, whether you have a fenced area and what you expect the dog to do for you. If you want the dog only for a pet many breeders will sell a dog on a limited AKC registration, which allows the dog to be entered in obedience trials but not conformation classes. It also prevents offspring from being registered with the AKC.

Serious dog breeders care very much where their puppies go. They want the puppies settled in a loving home for life. They want the relationship to be a secure, loving one that will bring joy to the owner and dog. Good dog breeders are also concerned about the dog population possibly exceeding the good homes available for dogs. They want to control excess population by informing people who do not know what they are getting into when they breed their pet. Generally, you want to find a breeder who is active in a local breed club, has had the parent's eyes and hips checked and is knowledgeable about genetic faults in the breed. People who show their dogs often can provide a puppy buyer with the guidance a new pet owner needs, because they are in the mainstream of the dog world. Hopefully, they are breeding the dogs with the important characteristics of the breed in mind. Backyard breeders generally

It's best to get your adorable puppy from a serious breeder, one who is knowledgeable about a breed's faults and wants every puppy to have a secure, loving home.

have no credentials of showing in conformation or obedience.
Those people who are vague as to the ancestry of their dogs
are usually not your best source for a puppy.

Puppies should be wormed regularly while they are with
their mother. They should also have their puppy shots. All
AKC-registered dogs should have registration papers available
to the new buyers, which may be limited registration papers or
full registration papers. Often, you will not be able to find the
puppy you want in your area, but dogs can be safely shipped
all over the world. A top quality pet or show puppy is often available and can be shipped to you by a recommended breeder. They also can often tell what puppy would suit you by asking a few questions about your family and lifestyle.

A good breeder will know every puppy intimately, helping to ensure that each is matched with the right owner.

A puppy's personality is shaped by genetics and interaction with his mother and littermates, yet each is unique.

MEETING PUPPIES

The sex of a Siberian is not as important as its personality. Many males are sweet, even-tempered, and easy to train and to handle. Some females are full of mischief and energy. An ultra-smart female can run circles around her cheerful, perhaps not so demanding, brother. Do not make your decision based solely on the sex of the puppy. It is best to visit the litter of puppies you are considering. Set a time to arrive and try to be punctual. If you are going to a kennel, the owners will have planned their routine work around your arrival. Often, puppies will be washed and brushed for you to see. You should have discussed what you want with the breeder before you arrive so he has a good idea of what puppy will fit your situation. If you are on time, and things are going as scheduled at the kennel, the pups should be clean and rested. Most breeders try to wash their puppies and give them time to calm down, eliminate and rest before people arrive. The breeder may have selected a couple of puppies to show you. Look at these and listen to the breeder's reasons why these were pre-selected for your viewing. If there are a number of puppies at the kennel, do not demand to see all of them. It is overwhelming for the prospective buyer to make sense out of a number of puppies. Often, all the puppies are not for sale.

Sometimes, buyers think there is a perfect puppy waiting for them, and they expect to know him when they see him. Generally, no bells will go off when a puppy walks into a room. How the puppy acts will depend on his age and how you act towards him. Fast, threatening gestures or loud noises tend to scare puppies. A six- to eight-week-old may simply sit and look over the new people. Especially if a large family group is

This six-and-one-half-week-old puppy shows she's not afraid of anything as she bounds through the door.

looking at a small puppy, he can be overwhelmed. Let him get used to this situation by sitting on the floor and speaking softly to him while holding him in your lap. In a few minutes he should relax and interact with you. Small children should sit as quietly as possible to avoid scaring the puppy. A ten- to sixteen-week-old puppy probably will come into the room full of energy, jumping all over you. Ten minutes or so and a little walk outside on a leash should settle him down.

It is usually more realistic to buy an older Siberian Husky puppy. Breeders often have a difficult time deciding which pup will be a show prospect and keep several for a period of time to evaluate them for show potential. A four-, six-, or eight-month-old puppy may be the right choice for you. Siberians will bond to most people who are receptive to them. They are very people-oriented dogs and bond to new owners at any age. A breeder's older puppy may have been leash trained, crate trained and started on housebreaking. Often, these

Born to be a sled dog. With lots of gentle exposure to people and things, this baby Husky will grow to be a well-adusted dog.

dogs make better behaved pets than an eight-week-old puppy. The older pup has learned a routine, and should be happy and well adjusted.

Sound genetics, socialization, lots of exposure to people, training and proper care are the things a dog needs to be well adjusted and to make a wonderful pet. The age is not as important as the way he has been handled and raised. The buyer should receive a pedigree of the puppy, an AKC registration paper (often called a blue slip), a health record of the puppy's immunizations and wormings, and feeding instructions. You should get answers to any questions that you have before you take the puppy home, and the breeder should be available by phone for routine questions after you have the puppy home.

CARING for Your Siberian Husky

A Siberian puppy grows rapidly. It is important that you train your puppy to become the adult dog you want him to be. You do not want your puppy to bark and whine when left alone, or chew on your furniture. You do want your puppy to come when called, and stand still for grooming and at the veterinarian's office. Remember, this puppy will be a 30- to 40-pound dog in a few months. Think about how "cute" his behavior will be when he is no longer a puppy. Training should start immediately.

Puppies have lots of energy and grow quickly. This one gets training and exercise going up and over a baby sliding board.

FEEDING

Feeding your Siberian properly primaily involves, in most cases, listening to your puppy's breeder. Feed the food that the puppy has been raised on since he began eating solid food. Siberians are efficient in digesting their food. Their metabolism system is unique. For their size, Siberians do not consume a large amount of food. However, they must be fed the correct diet for them or they will have loose stools (diarrhea) and even develop mineral deficiencies. Most cases of diarrhea in Siberians are due to improper diet or internal parasites, coccidiosis or giardiasis. Parasites, coccidiosis or giardiasis require treatment by your veterinarian.

Correct diet is something that you can easily control. Puppies are like babies, the best food for them is the food they are used to and that agrees with them. Siberians need a high-protein, high-fat, highly digestible dog food. The main source

34

From the time puppies are weaned off their mother's milk, they need well-balanced, nutritious foods. These pups chow down on a special blend prepared by their breeder. of protein must be from animals, not plants. Make sure there is no soy in the food. Siberians do not digest soy products very well, and food containing soy will cause loose stools.

Dog food is a big business and many of the food companies are constantly trying to convince the owners that their food is best. There are many good dog foods on the market, but many of the foods that are acceptable for other breeds are not suitable for Siberians. Since Siberians consume a relatively small quantity of food for their size, they must have a high-quality, highly digestible food. The digestibility of most dog foods on the market is not of a high enough quality to work well for Siberian puppies. A chicken-based, high-protein, high-fat, top-of-the-line dog food from any of the major companies is what a growing Siberian puppy needs.

We do not feed our puppies puppy food. Many puppy foods have milk or whey added, are lower in protein and cause the puppy to have loose stools. Loose stools on a new puppy play havoc with housebreaking and result in slower growth and poor condition. Many new owners will change foods trying to cure the problem, and this causes stomach irritation, and the problem escalates. Veterinarians often prescribe many of the new special diets on the market with little success.

PREVENTING DIARRHEA

If your Siberian puppy has loose stools after you bring him home, here are some things to try:

1. Take a stool sample to the veterinarian and have it checked for parasites, including coccidiosis and giardiasis. If the stool sample tests negative, take a second sample; about 50 percent of the time parasite eggs are not present in the stool even though the puppy has the parasite.

2. Double-check what you're feeding your puppy. Is it exactly the same food as the breeder told you to feed? For example, if the breeder suggested a top-of-the-line brand and you are feeding the puppy a maintenance mixture, it is not the same food.

3. Do not feed dog treats or table scraps to young puppies. The recipe for dog treats can be very different from the dog's regular food. Give the puppy a piece of his regular dog food as a treat.

4. Some of the hickory treated rawhides are too much of a good thing for a greedy puppy, as are bones. Nylabones® are best.

5. Check and see if your puppy is drinking an unusual amount of water. Sometimes when a puppy is shipped to a hot climate or has been deprived of water, he may drink water excessively. This is a difficult problem to correct. The puppy needs an adequate amount of water, but if he is just drinking water as a nervous reaction, substitute ice cubes for some of the water. Chewing on the cubes may satisfy his obsession for water and he will not drink so frantically.

6. Feed your puppy several small meals of dry dog food a day. If he eats small amounts often, he does not overload his stomach and will want smaller amounts of water at a time. Large meals followed by large amounts of water cause loose stools.

7. Two hours after a dog eats, he usually drinks his largest amount of water. Consider your feeding times to coincide with his need for water. Also, allow him to eliminate at about this time.

8. Many times, temporary relief can be obtained by giving the puppy an antacid. This is an over-the-counter medicine and the dosage recommended for a 9- to 12-year-old child is adequate for a puppy.

GROOMING

Most Siberian breeders or owners advocate grooming. So the question is, How should we groom our dogs, why, when and how often?

All Siberians should be frequently groomed, bathed and brushed from the time they are small puppies. The grooming process teaches the baby Siberians to be comfortable being handled and worked with. It's preferable to start the puppy on a table with a non-skid surface on it. Using a table gives the owner an advantage over the dog. The dog will

Puppies are curious creatures who will investigate anything - especially if it smells good! Getting into the feed bag and overeating could cause digestive upset, so supervise your pup.

not struggle to get away as much if he has the boundaries of the table to deal with. If you groom on the floor, it is difficult for the puppy to know the difference between play time and grooming time.

An eight-week-old puppy should be put on the table and brushed for a few moments with a slicker brush each day. Pick up his feet, look in his ears and check his teeth. Talk to him and tell him that he is a good puppy. This routine, done regularly, lets your puppy associate good feelings with being groomed. Routine shampooing of your dog can be done with regular dishwashing liquid soap diluted with water. One part soap to three parts water seems to be the best combination. Some people feel that a soap with lemon scent has a beneficial effect on the dog's coat. You must rinse the dog's coat completely to remove all soap, then towel dry or use a hair dryer.

When a Siberian sheds his hair, aggressive grooming is required. A rake, Greyhound-type comb and slicker brush are necessary tools for grooming a Siberian at this time. If the dog has been bathed regularly, blown out with a cool air dryer and brushed while you blow the hair out, you will not have as much hair to remove during this shedding period. Use your rake and comb when the dog first starts shedding. Siberians do not generally shed all of their hair at one time. You will see puffs of hair start on the legs and thighs at the beginning of the shedding season. The body goes into a shed in the second stage of shedding. The last areas of the body hair to loosen up are the britches and tail areas. The neck and chest areas take plenty of work to get all the old hair out. Warm baths throughout the shedding season, combined with raking and combing the hair out, shorten the period when the dog is losing hair. Without an aggressive grooming schedule, the dog will be losing hair for several weeks.

When your Husky's shedding, you can even run the slicker brush through his coat while you give him a bath to pull out more hair.

When bathing your Husky, put him on a non-slip surface where you can wet his coat to the skin and really work in the shampoo.

EXERCISE

Exercise for the wonderful Siberian can take many forms. Exercise for the dog is play time, preferably with you. It is a natural bonding, training, fun time for you and your Siberian. If you have a fenced-in yard, play with him in this area. Siberians are not natural retrievers; however, they do like to chase a Frisbee® or a ball for a while. Don't expect them to bring it back to you unless they feel like it. Siberians also love to jump. Jumping on and off a picnic table or over a barrel is a wonderful game for them. Freestyle play to take the edge off their exuberant nature very naturally leads into some semi-serious training time. After a few minutes of running around chasing things, bring out the training leash and collar and do some on-leash work with the heel, sit, stay and come commands. Make it fun, use a firm but positive tone of voice. A few minutes a day of working together from the time you bring your Siberian into your home will develop a bond between you. Your Siberian will learn from an early age that there is a time to work and a time to play. He will listen to you and anticipate what you want him to do.

Going for a walk is great for your Siberian and yourself. Check out the neighborhood. A Flexi-lead works well for spaces where he can range freely but also must, at times, be close to you. Jogging suits Siberians to a tee. One Siberian owner in Florida jogs at 4:30 a.m. daily with his two Siberians. He has told me that it is quite a challenge to jog with two Siberians, each on his own Flexi-lead.

Riding a bicycle with an attachment to keep the dog running alongside the bike is very popular with Siberian owners. This exercise is not for the faint of heart, but it is wonderful for dog and owner.

Siberians are endurance running dogs. Like all athletes, they must be conditioned to perform for extended periods of time. Temperature and humidity should be evaluated when you are exercising your dog. You must also consider the surface that your dog is running on. The pads of his feet can quickly become sore and tender if you are on concrete or blacktop, although grass or sand surfaces seem to cause no problems. You must check your dog's feet often to be sure that the hard surface he is

Huskies thrive on regular exercise and love everything from jogging to playing to swimming - and sledding, of course.

running on is not wearing the pads. If his feet are worn down, red or sore-looking, rest him for a few days and then walk him on grass or sand. Dog racers use "booties" on tender feet. These are usually made of polar fleece material and are available through specialty dog sledding equipment catalogs.

The real issue of how much exercise your Siberian needs is not in hours or miles but in how much time you have to spend bonding with him. Your Siberian needs you to be his companion and advisor–his parent, if you will. Your Siberian is very bright, energetic, and eager to learn. If you make this dog a part of your life, he will adapt to a great variance in the amount of exercise he needs. Your Siberian can be conditioned like the athlete he his is to run with a marathon runner or to walk with a person who goes at a slower pace. The same principles apply to the dog as to the man. Regular conditioning, gradual increase in distance and speed, and consideration for temperature, humidity and surface condition must all be evaluated in your exercise program. Your Siberian can also adapt to a more sedentary lifestyle, but his intake of food must be adjusted accordingly.

You and your Husky will enjoy a good romp across a big field.

SPECIAL ACTIVITIES FOR YOUR HUSKY

The Siberian is a highly intelligent, alert animal with an inquiring mind. The Siberian can be trained to do many things. His fame as a working sled dog is legendary.

Siberians love to work on a sled, their enthusiasm is unlimited. They run on the sled because they want to run, not because they are being forced to run. Many Siberian owners enjoy running their dogs. Three Siberians are usually needed to make up a small team. Dog sled racers and explorers use larger teams—as many as 15 to 20 dogs—to pull heavy loads or go long distances. The most challenging aspect of sledding is to find a dog that will lead the team. The dogs behind the leader instinctively take to running in harness. Finding and training a dog to act as a leader is much more difficult. The lead dog can be trained by putting his harness on him and attaching it to a line that is secured to a small tire. The owner runs alongside the dog with a leash on the dog's collar and encourages him to go forward and to turn to the right or left. You are teaching the dog to pull something behind him as well as obey commands. Reassure the dog that it is okay to have this strange object behind him. Run along with the dog until he learns to pull and is not afraid of the tire. Teach the dog his commands: "GEE" for a right turn, "HAW" for a left turn, and "WHOA" to stop.

Several books are available on sled dog training. Carts, sleds, harnesses and other specialized equipment are available through specialty catalogs. Do not have your dog pull anything with his collar, and never use a choke chain when doing this type of training. Dogs that pull need a properly fitted harness. A sled

Author Kathleen Kanzler gets ready to take her team for a run in New York state. Huskies take naturally to this kind of activity.

You will love hiking with your Husky, especially when he can carry his own backpack, like this one does.

or cart needs a brake so that neither runs up on the dog and injures or frightens him.

A single Siberian can be trained to skijor; that is, pull the owner while he is on skis. A line is attached from the dog's harness to the person on skis. This resembles a person water-skiing, but the boat is replaced by your dog and the water skis by cross country skis. Cross country skiers find this a wonderful sport in which to participate with their dogs.

Siberians can also carry a backpack on camping trips or day hikes. A dog backpack is actually two packs, one falling on each side of the dog's back. Dog packs must fit a dog properly. A young dog should have a very light pack—perhaps just the dog's water and snacks. The load carried by a dog in a pack should never exceed one-half of the dog's weight and even that weight should only be carried when the dog has been properly trained and conditioned. Care must be taken to fit the pack properly and weigh the loaded pack before you put it on the dog. The weight of the pack should be evenly distributed on both sides. Terrain and length of the hike must be calculated so the dog is not overloaded.

Siberians, with their outgoing, friendly natures, are naturals for therapy dog work. Many Siberians are registered therapy dogs. This is a very rewarding activity for an owner with a well-trained, sociable Siberian. Hospitals, schools and retirement homes utilize therapy dogs in their patients' activities. Social workers schedule the dogs to come and visit with the patients. Many of these people miss the companionship of a dog, and it is a rewarding experience to see your Siberian bring a smile to a patient's face.

HOUSING YOUR SIBERIAN OUTDOORS

Where should you keep your Siberian puppy if all the members of the household work outside the home? Not on a line, which some people refer to as a dog run. The best place to put your wonderful Siberian is in a portable chain-link dog pen. He will be safe there in the fresh air, be able to get exercise, and will not destroy your house while you are away. Portable chain-link dog runs are available from local fence companies, building supply companies and farm centers. The size pen for an adult Siberian is 6 feet wide by 12 feet long by 6 feet high.

These so called "portable" fences are panels of framed pipe with chain-link fabric stretched into the pipe. One panel has a gate in it. The framed panels clamp together on site to make a fenced enclosure for your Siberian. The kennel run must be on an easy-to-clean surface, ideally of poured concrete. If pouring a slab of concrete, slope the slab one inch per foot in the direction you want the water to run off the slab. An alternative is to use 2-foot by 2-foot patio blocks set closely together in sand. Give yourself two feet of slab in front of the gate to access the kennel run. The slab should extend slightly beyond the perimeters of the fence so that the fence panels sit solidly on the hard surface to prevent your dog from digging out.

Tie down every square of chain link to the metal pipe with metal ties to prevent dogs from escaping through the bottom of the fence. The hard surface for the dog run is essential. Grass turns to dirt and mud immediately, and dogs will dig out just as quickly. An alternative to concrete is concrete squares in gravel. If this is used, railroad ties must be placed around all four sides of the enclosure. The chain-link panels should be placed on top of the railroad ties, and the gravel should go inside them.

It is best to lay down chain link a little past the outer edges of your fence, then put railroad ties or cement block in the exact measurement and shape as the portable dog run, which will sit on top of them. Fill the run with gravel, with the chain link under the gravel. The perimeter should be lined with railroad ties or cement block. This effectively prevents the dog from digging out.

Another kennel option for people in very busy neighborhoods is to have the dog kennel run inside a garage and use wood shavings on the floor to soak up any mess. This set-up protects the dog from the weather and neighborhood dogs and children. In the summer you can put a fan in the window and keep the air cool and comfortable.

Consideration should be given to placement of the dog run for your convenience and the comfort of the dog. Situating the run near a rear door is convenient when exercising the dog in the dark or cold. A run attached to a garage is also a good arrangement. Section off a small interior area (3' x 3') with fence panels. This area is the dog's inside quarters when he

Proper outdoor housing consists of well-constructed pens large enough for the dogs to run and play in, shady areas, and fun toys like this boat the puppies can climb on.

45

has to be left alone. Install a dog door in the garage wall to give the puppy access to his outside run. The dog should utilize the area in the garage as he would the house. He should eliminate in the outside run and use the inside for sleeping or hanging out in bad weather. Provide a sleeping platform or a doghouse in this inside run.

If the dog run is entirely outside, a good doghouse and a sun screen over the entire run are essential. Fabric sun screen is sized and sold with grommets similar to tarps. Either tarps or sun screens can be used. In climates with heavy snow a solid roof is necessary. Dogs cannot be kept in the sun without shade. It's absolutely necessary that there be shade for your Siberian Husky. No dog can take direct sunlight for a whole day, especially a dog like the Siberian whose ancestors may have only seen the sun for a few hours a day!

THE DOGHOUSE

What kind of doghouse is best for a Siberian? You can build a house from one sheet of exterior plywood. Siberians love the flat roof of this kind of house. In the biggest snow storm they will lay on top of their house in utter contentment.

If you wish to build a commercial plastic doghouse choose a heavy-duty model. The dogs will easily chew up the light plastic models, so invest in the heavier construction. If you use a wooden doghouse make sure the paint or varnish you use to finish it is non-toxic to your dog. Spray the inside of the

Dogs need access to fresh, cool water at all times of the day. Change the water often, especially if your dog puts more than his mouth in it.

doghouse with one of the many products on the market which will discourage chewing.

Siberians are not a particularly destructive breed of dog. Siberians are very sociable, smart dogs. When any dog is left alone for a long period of time, it will look for something to do to amuse itself. If all it has available to play with is a doghouse, it will chew on the house. Give him some toys that he can play with and chew on.

ELECTRONIC FENCES

These "fenceless" fences can work for Siberians as a secondary fence. This type of containment is not suitable as a

A safe, strong Nylabone® Wishbone will satisfy your Husky's need to chew indoors or out.

primary fence for a Siberian. It is no fence. The radio collar the dog wears emits a warning beep when he enters a programmed area near the buried electric wire. The dog is supposed to turn around and leave the danger area. The Siberian may or may not do so.

Siberians are free spirits. They have a sense of humor and an intelligence level above or at least different from other dogs. Siberians do not want to run away so much as they want to meet a challenge. Several situations may occur. They may become frightened by the shock collar and run through the boundary area, see an animal or another dog to play with, or just work themselves up to take the pain and go through the barrier area.

The radio collar/buried fence system can work well depending on certain situations as a secondary fence. This fence can be successful in a rural area when the owner is out with the dog. If the owner is working in the yard, the dog will be happy to stay in this type of fence. This type of fence is not suitable as a primary fence for a Siberian left alone all day.

TRAINING Your Siberian Husky

Start training your puppy the first day you bring him home. Your priority will be to housebreak your puppy. Everything you do with your puppy should be a positive learning experience. Give the new puppy the time and opportunity to relieve himself before you bring him into the house for the first time. Confine the puppy to the kitchen area by using a baby gate to close off other parts of the house. Your mission is to acclimate this puppy to his new home in an orderly and calm fashion.

Baby gates are valuable aids to housebreaking and training, confining your puppy to rooms where he can't make too much of a mess.

Take the new puppy outside for the first few hours every 15 minutes. Take him out the same door to the same spot in the yard or into his fenced dog run. Select the spot you want him to use. When he has eliminated, praise him and return to the house. Do not give the puppy the freedom of the house. Put the puppy on a leash and collar if you want to take him into other areas of your home. With the puppy on a leash, you have control and you remain aware of where the puppy is and what he is doing. If you want the puppy with you while you watch television, or visit with family or friends, put him on his leash. You can correct him quickly if he gets into something inappropriate. Plants, shoes, waste baskets, rugs, all kinds of items that may be on the floor are off limits to the puppy. If you have him on a leash, you can give it a tug and say no in a firm voice. When he leaves the item alone, praise him and pet him.

With a positive early experience, your dog will look upon his crate as a safe den where he can go to rest and relax.

The goal is to have a puppy who is immediately housebroken. Many people report that they have no "accidents" or only one or two with their new Siberian. The breed as a whole is smart and wants to be clean in the house. To do that the dog has to have a smart owner, one who is time-conscious and realizes that a new puppy needs to go out every few minutes for the first day or two in a new home.

As the puppy becomes more used to his new environment, he relaxes and does not need to go out to relieve himself so often. Exiting by the same door from the same room that the puppy thinks of as his home is a big step in housebreaking. At this time, you are also putting the puppy in his crate for a few minutes when you bring him in from outside. Just a few minutes in a crate will familiarize him to this new way of life. Remember, do not let him scream and carry on in the crate. Insist that he be quiet and let him out when he is quiet, if only for a moment. This inside-outside routine with the few minutes in the crate throughout the day will be a major step in establishing the puppy's daily routine and teaching him how to be clean in your home.

Always exercise your dog before you put him in the crate. Use newspapers as bedding in case of an accident. Towels and rugs are fuel for a puppy's sharp little teeth and may end up in his tiny stomach and cause serious problems. For the first few nights that your puppy is with you, move the crate to your bedroom. Put the puppy to bed when you go to bed. You may give him a safe chewing device to play with, such as a Gumabone®. If the puppy cries after you turn out the light, reassure him quietly or tap the top of the crate with your fingers. After a busy day, he should be tired and ready to sleep.

The first few nights that you have your puppy, he may need to relieve himself before you get up in the morning. The puppy will wake up and cry frantically to get out of his crate. Take the puppy out of the crate and carry him outside. Do not open the door and let him follow you because he will probably have an accident on the floor before you get him outside. You are responding to your puppy's frantic need to relieve himself. His instinct is to not soil the place he sleeps. Hopefully, he will not relieve himself on you as you are carrying him outside. After the puppy has relieved himself outside, bring him back inside and put him back in the crate. You may have a little more trouble getting him to go back to sleep, but if you comfort him and praise him, he will eventually drift off.

After the first few days you should have observed the signs your puppy will give you when he needs to go out to "exercise," or relieve himself. He may go and look at the door. He may stop playing and put his nose to the floor and circle, looking for a place to relieve himself. Immediately pick him up and take him outside. Praise him when he's finished and return with him to the house.

This focus on your puppy pays off very well. You should have a housebroken puppy in a short time and no damage to your rugs and furniture. Gradually, let him have access to the other rooms in the house. Use your baby gate to prohibit entry to selected rooms.

It is not recommended to papertrain a puppy in the house first and then housebreak him outside. Dogs are creatures of habit. They learn one thing and learn it well. You have to go through the entire procedure again to train him from papers to the outdoors. Fortunately, weather is not a consideration with this breed. Siberian puppies of eight weeks or more are well-suited to using the outdoors to relieve themselves, regardless of the temperature.

CRATE TRAINING

The most important thing in starting out with a new Siberian puppy or adult is to have a place for him to live. You want a house dog, a companion for you and your family. The accommodations you provide for your dog make the difference between enjoying your dog and having to replace him because he does not fit into your lifestyle. Crate training is not cruel.

Puppies who aren't confined to a puppy-proofed room or a crate can get in all kinds of trouble - it's the owner's responsibility to keep accidents like this from happening.

Just as people choose to protect their human babies by using a crib and playpen, a dog crate and dog run serve the same purpose for puppies. The wire crate must be strong and have a good door and latches.

Do not try to save money when purchasing a crate: your dog's safety is the price you will pay for being frugal. Siberians can be determined when they want to change their place or situation and it is not unusual for them to escape from a flimsy wire crate or dog fence. Quality manufacturers build stronger, more escape-proof crates and pet shops usually carry an excellent selection of these. Discuss with the proprietor which size you'll need to house the adult Siberian Husky. Purchase the size you'll need for the adult dog and section it off so that the puppy cannot misuse the crate. The crate is for sleeping and relaxing, the puppy shouldn't be able to piddle on one side and sleep on the other. Some crates are collapsible and can fold down into the size of a large suitcase for easy storage or travel in vehicles.

The crate size for most adult Siberians is 36 inches long, 24 inches wide and 26 inches high. The dog crate may be made of plastic, an airline-type crate, or of wire. Wire crates usually fold flat when not in use, and plastic crates can bolt together in the middle. The upper half turned over fits inside the bottom with the wire door fitting between the two halves for storage. The dissembled plastic crate will fit in the trunk of many cars and can be used for luggage when traveling. When you arrive at your destination, the crate can be reassembled quickly to accommodate your dog.

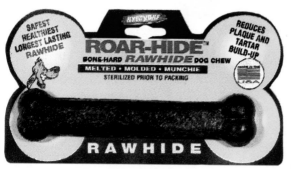

The Roarhide® is a molded rawhide by Nylabone that dogs love for the taste and owners love because it's safe and keeps a puppy occupied.

The dog crate is a tool to use throughout your dog's life, and acclimating your puppy to his crate takes time and patience. Naturally the puppy would rather be playing with you and wants to be free to do whatever he wants, but he must learn to stay quietly in different places and not be destructive. No one is able to supervise his dog 24 hours a day.

All dogs enjoy having a soft, padded mat or bed to sleep on. Make sure there's one in the crate with your puppy.

Basic crate training is the beginning of a busy learning time for you and your new Siberian. Always exercise the puppy outside before you crate him, then make a game of spending quiet time in the crate. As you work around the house, put your Siberian in his crate for a few minutes several times a day. Close the door and give him a Nylabone® to play with. When he complains about being in the crate, tell him "No" loudly and tap on the top of the crate with your fingers. He does not have to stay in the crate for a long time. The secret of crate training is to only let him out when he is quiet—except of course when he needs to go outside to relieve himself. The one moment he is quiet, let him out of the crate. Also, use the crate in the house as a "time out" place for your puppy. When you have delivery men or repairmen in your home, put the puppy in his crate where he will be safe. You can be sure that he is not running out an open door into traffic if he is safely in his crate.

The crate is a basic accessory for your dog. You can use it anytime your dog needs a break from visiting children who are not treating your dog properly, or to give your visitors who may be afraid of dogs a break.

Now that I have convinced you that crate training is good for your dog, I am going to tell you not to leave him in the crate all day! The crate is to be used only for short periods of time and at night, or as long as it takes to housetrain your Siberian completely. The crate is not to be used as a prison. Puppies cannot be crated day and night. They must have the opportunity to go outside to relieve themselves and to run and play outdoors.

TRAINING

The key to happily cohabitating with a Siberian is to properly train the dog. Siberians are adept at taking advantage of the situation and trying to train you! Do not let your dog run wild in the house. Watch your puppy as you would a two-year-old child. Do not leave him unsupervised when you are busy with a project or in the shower. If you're unable to watch him, put him in his crate or outside in his dog run.

The more time you spend showing your puppy the world and letting her know the rules, the better adjusted she will be as an adult.

Any problem you prevent by good management of your Siberian you will be repaid by immeasurably. Dogs do not need to have their own way in your world. They can learn to be good citizens and adjust to the routine of others. When you say "NO" to your dog, mean it. Do not nag him but be firm and distract him with a chew toy or other activity. Do not let him engage in activities that cause you more work or cause harm to you or your belongings. Use your voice in a stern manner to let your Siberian know his behavior is unacceptable. If that does not cause him to stop unwanted behavior such as jumping on furniture, eating plants or emptying wastebaskets, resort to sterner measures.

At our kennel, we are very physical with our puppies. By this I mean we pick them up a lot and handle them from the time they are born. We stroke them, look in their mouths and talk to them from birth. At four to six weeks of age, we pick them up gently, sometimes by the scruff of the neck, and pet them. This familiarizes the puppy with people's hands and with being handled in a variety of ways. During this time period, and later, we take each puppy and restrain him on his side while he is laying on our lap. We do not do this in a frightening manner. We speak to the puppy in a soothing tone. A puppy may struggle and cry to be put down to play, but this is a very important lesson to learn. Every dog must learn respect; each one must learn to listen to you and submit to your handling. When the puppy relaxes and lays quietly on our lap, we praise him and put him down to play. We never hit or spank the puppy. Puppies do not understand this type of correction. They understand the same types of correction their mothers used on them. Holding the puppy and giving it

Free-spirited Huskies get ideas of their own. You may want to stage a situation in which your pup misbehaves so you can correct him while he's in the act.

physical contact is something a new owner should make part of an everyday training routine. This also reinforces the puppy's role with the owner, which is that it must listen and do what the person wants.

We humans may not be the masters of our free-spirited Siberian Huskies; however, we can be their boss. Set up training situations to prevent problems as well as correct bad habits. Obedience trainers don't wait for a situation to happen and react to it, they stage situations to train the dog at a time and place when they can deal with his behavior properly. As a new or prospective Siberian owner, you need to look to the future and take the same approach to training your puppy.

Dogs should let you take things out of their mouths. This sounds like a simplistic statement, but many new dog owners are horrified when their sweet puppy growls at them when they reach to take a toy or something inappropriate away from the puppy. Don't let this happen. Do not let a confrontation between you and your dog occur. Set up a training routine from day one. Talk to your puppy while you are handling him. During feeding time, speak to the puppy so he knows you are there, hold him by the collar with one hand and pick up his dish of food with the other hand. Say "wait," release and praise the puppy and return the dish to the floor. By initiating these training situations with your puppy, you are in control. You are training him to let you do to him whatever you want.

If your pup has taken an item you do not want him to have under a piece of furniture, do not try to pull the item from his mouth. The puppy's instinct is to guard his trophy. It is not a sign of poor temperament. If possible, move the piece of furniture. Put a leash on the puppy or take hold of the collar to pull him out of his "den," but do not grab the item in his mouth. Then, holding the puppy by the back of his neck, push his lips over his teeth to make him open his mouth and remove the item. Praise him and give him a toy he is allowed to play with.

To prevent possessiveness over the food bowl, interact with your dog during mealtimes from the time she's a puppy.

Along with his food dish, you should regularly take a puppy's toy away from him so he understands that you are the boss and that he must never challenge your right to take things he is playing with. Hold onto his collar so you have control, remove the item from his mouth, say "Out", and praise him for being such a good dog. There are many times in a dog's life when you will need to take a dangerous item away from him. He should learn to drop an item when you say "Out" and let you take the most wonderful trophy, a bird, sharp item, etc., from him at your vocal command.

57

HUSKIES AND OTHER ANIMALS

Siberians are pack animals, and as a breed socialize well with other dogs. An important part of your daily training is to introduce your inquisitive Siberian puppy to his new world. A Siberian naturally likes company. A dog friend is an exciting prospect for him and your puppy may be wildly excited upon meeting a new dog. He had been used to playing with his littermates and may have been surrounded by other dogs if he was raised in a kennel. In this situation, you will have to direct his behavior in an appropriate manner. Keep him away from aggressive dogs and introduce him to dogs that seem friendly. Watch and supervise these dogs closely. A puppy will fawn over and be submissive to an older dog, often licking his face. Some older dogs will bite a puppy. Don't let your puppy get into a situation where he can become injured or badly frightened.

The alert, eagle-eyed Siberian will see every cat, rabbit and squirrel in the area. Their first reaction will be one of interest. Your Siberian should not be aggressive to other animals. Start training him to accept these other creatures when you are walking your Siberian puppy. When he sees another animal, let him look at it. When he goes to chase it or pounce on it, say an extremely firm "NO" and use a strong leash correction.

Many dog owners have cats and dogs together, living as friends in their home. If you are bringing a puppy into a home where there is a cat, prepare the cat. Bring the puppy into the house on a leash. Let the cat see that you have a dog with you. Do not let the puppy near the cat while the cat is on the floor. Give the cat time to jump up on something out of the puppy's reach. Most puppies have too many other things to check out in their new home and do not focus their attention on a cat that is sitting above floor level. If for some reason the puppy does focus on the cat and repeatedly tries to reach the cat (which is more likely to happen with an older puppy or adult dog), correct the Siberian sternly. The cat often can do more damage to the puppy, especially if it scratches the puppy's eyes, than the puppy can do trying to chase the cat. Cats, when they have been forewarned about a dog in the house, will stay out of the dog's reach for several days. Do not force the issue of the dog and cat interacting. Cats cannot be forced to socialize with a dog. After a few days, a cat will accept the situation. When the cat realizes the dog is living in his home, he will adjust his life around the dog. It is up to you to monitor their behavior. The dog should be trained to leave the cat alone. Very stern "NOs," leash corrections and, if he is persistent, scruff shakes should cure him of inappropriate behavior such as running after, chasing or jumping for the cat. Different species, dogs and cats, will work out a peaceable living arrangement.

The entire focus of starting out with your new Siberian companion is to think ahead and mold this exuberant, intelligent animal into a well-behaved canine citizen. Siberians, like any breed of dog, need guidance and training to reach their full potential. This means there will be times when, while you are raising this very intelligent, calculating dog, your wills will clash. Siberians have active minds and some of the "too-smart" Huskies appear to have reasoning powers beyond most dogs. I would not classify the Siberian Husky as a stubborn breed of dog; rather, as very determined. They are not easily discouraged when they want to do something. The mental toughness that makes them run, work and

A Nylafloss® and beautiful weather are all these puppies need to get the exercise their growing bodies need.

persevere in incredible winter conditions are traits that a Siberian owner must understand to properly train the breed.

Siberians do not respond to physical punishment. Dog drivers are not successful in force-training Siberians to run on the sled. Siberian pet owners must be strong-minded and consistent in training the breed. A calm routine with an attitude of trying to see how the dog views the situation will result in success. At some point, you may have to impose your will on his desire to do something. If he is repeatedly defying you—for example, if he will not go into his crate when you tell him, or if he barks excessively or jumps on things or people—shake him up. Use your hands and your voice in an authoritative manner to get your point across. This method is not for puppies. Adolescent dogs and young adults that do not respect you need a quick, short lesson in proper behavior.

When a Siberian or any breed gets to a stage where he is obnoxious and disregards firm, patient training, it is time to change tactics. Step up your obedience training routine. Take your Siberian out and do leash training routines for 15 minutes or more. Keep him on the leash in the house. If he is wild in the house, tie him to a door knob or heavy piece of furniture. Do not let him be obnoxious. If you have worked properly with your Siberian puppy from the beginning, you should not have to resort to excessive methods of training.

If you are reading this book for help in retraining a dog that has not been properly trained, do not give up on him. Good habits can be taught and bad habits can be corrected. A Siberian is very intelligent. If you project your will over his and insist on good behavior, he will adjust. Most Siberians are

realists, and do not hold grudges. If you change the ground rules, they will adapt to those changes and respect you.

It takes firm, consistent training to teach your dog to be a well-mannered companion.

Dogs should be taught to sit while being greeted. This puppy is learning from two teachers—a well-behaved adult dog and her owner.

CHECK LIST FOR NEW PUPPIES

Lesson One: Take puppy outside to relieve himself when he first awakes, after he has eaten, and after playing hard.

Lesson Two: Think ahead with all of your interactions with your new puppy. It's certainly cute when your puppy is so happy to see you he jumps all over you with joy. This bond between a dog and his family is why you got a dog. However, think ahead to the times you might come in to the house in your dress clothes or have little children with you. Then it may not be so nice to have your dog jumping for joy when you come in. Teach your Siberian to sit before you pet him. Sit in a chair and call the puppy to you. Speak in a happy voice. Reach for his collar with one hand, pull him forward as you tell him to sit and push on his hindquarters with your other hand. The puppy will sit. Repeat this a couple of times.

Praise the puppy. Tell him how smart he is and how quickly he is learning his new skill. Repeat the routine several times a day. Make the puppy sit when someone comes into the house, then bend over and greet the dog. Dogs want to see your face and spend time greeting you when you have been away. Start out teaching them the appropriate way to greet people and you will not have to stop the dog from jumping on you when he weighs forty pounds.

Lesson Three: Leash training your puppy starts the moment you obtain him. Use a buckle collar. Do not use choke chains on puppies or young dogs. Check the collar to be sure it is tight enough so the puppy cannot back out of it and get loose, which can be very dangerous. If he backs out of his collar in traffic, it can be fatal. Also, check the collar to make sure it is not too tight, and do so periodically to see that the puppy isn't growing faster than you expected.

The initial leash training should be done by a responsible adult. Hopefully, the breeder will have had the puppy started on a leash and collar. Place your puppy on the ground with his leash and collar on and

This Husky clears an obedience-trial high jump with room to spare. Watching your dog perform this or other feats achievable through training is one of the joys of owning a dog.

62

let him walk around. Go with him until he gets used to this strange restriction around his neck. Do not force him to go with you. Go his way, talking and encouraging the puppy to stay next to your left leg.

Purchase a retractable leash. This leash is a popular way of giving the dog more exercise and playtime while you are walking or jogging with your dog. The leash extends a number of feet and then retracts when you push a button.

Dogs love the feeling of freedom the retractable leash gives them. It is also an excellent way to start teaching your Siberian to come when called.

Lesson Four: While the puppy is relieving himself outside, use a phrase to teach him when to go to the bathroom. Many people will say words such as "Hurry, hurry" or "Do your business" while the dog is urinating or defecating. Afterwards praise the dog. This will train the dog to know the difference between taking a sightseeing walk and a quick bathroom jaunt before bedtime.

Leash training should start early and be an enjoyable experience for young dogs, like this group of Innisfree puppies.

ADVANCED TRAINING

Obedience training is a necessary activity for your smart and active Siberian. Incorporate the training previously described in this chapter and attend classes to do advanced obedience work. Enroll your new puppy in puppy kindergarten classes to make training a happy experience from the start—a type of game you play with your dog. Be realistic about what you expect from your puppy, but insist on basic good behavior. Buy a training book and follow the program outlined in it. Be fair and consistent in your dealings with this new and very important member of your family. Remember, Siberians consider you more of a friend than a master. Laugh a lot with this animated, sometimes super-charged Siberian and have a great life together.

SPORT of Purebred Dogs

Welcome to the exciting and sometimes frustrating sport of dogs. No doubt you are trying to learn more about dogs or you wouldn't be deep into this book. This section covers the basics that may entice you, further your knowledge and help you to understand the dog world. If you decide to give showing, obedience or any other dog activities a try, then I suggest you seek further help from the appropriate source.

Dog showing has been a very popular sport for a long time and has been taken quite seriously by some. Others only enjoy it as a hobby.

The Kennel Club in England was formed in 1859, the American Kennel Club was established in 1884 and the Canadian Kennel Club was formed in 1888. The purpose of these clubs was to register purebred dogs and maintain their Stud Books. In the beginning, the concept of registering dogs was not readily accepted. More than 36 million dogs have been enrolled in the AKC Stud Book since its inception in 1888. Presently the kennel clubs not only register dogs but adopt and enforce rules and regulations governing dog shows, obedience trials and field trials. Over the years they have fostered and encouraged interest in the health and welfare of the purebred dog. They routinely donate funds to veterinary research for study on genetic disorders.

Below are the addresses of the kennel clubs in the United States, Great Britain and Canada.

The American Kennel Club
51 Madison Avenue
New York, NY 10010

Their registry is located at:
5580 Centerview Drive, STE 200
Raleigh, NC 27606-3390

The Kennel Club
1 Clarges Street
Piccadilly, London, WIY 8AB, England

The Canadian Kennel Club
111 Eglinton Avenue
East Toronto, Ontario M6S 4V7
Canada

Conformation shows are just one of many sports in which people and their dogs can participate.

Today there are numerous activities that are enjoyable for both the dog and the handler. Some of the activities include conformation showing, obedience competition, tracking, agility, the Canine Good Citizen

Certificate, and a wide range of instinct tests that vary from breed to breed. Where you start depends upon your goals, which early on may not be readily apparent.

PUPPY KINDERGARTEN

Every puppy will benefit from this class. PKT is the foundation for all future dog activities from conformation to "couch potatoes." Pet owners should make an effort to attend even if they never expect to show their dog. The class is designed for puppies about three months of age with graduation at approximately five months of age. All the puppies will be in the same age group and, even though some may be a little unruly, there should not be any real problem. This class will teach the puppy some beginning obedience. As in all obedience classes the owner learns how to train his own dog. The PKT class gives the puppy the opportunity to interact with other puppies in the same age group and exposes him to strangers,

Puppies learn a lot by playing with each other—their littermates and strangers, too. That's why puppy kindergarten is so beneficial.

"Sit" is probably the command you will use the most with your dog. It tells him to plant his butt and relax for a bit. which is very important. Some dogs grow up with behavior problems, one of them being fear of strangers. As you can see, there can be much to gain from this class.

There are some basic obedience exercises that every dog should learn. Some of these can be started with puppy kindergarten.

Sit

One way of teaching the sit is to have your dog on your left side with the leash in your right hand, close to the collar. Pull up on the leash and at the same time reach around his hindlegs with your left hand and tuck them in. As you are doing this say, "Beau, sit." Always use the dog's name when you give an active command. Some owners like to use a treat, holding it over the dog's head. The dog will need to sit to get the treat. Encourage the dog to hold the sit for a few seconds, which will eventually be the beginning of the Sit/Stay. Depending on how cooperative he is, you can rub him under the chin or stroke his back. It is a good time to establish eye contact.

Down

Sit the dog on your left side and kneel down beside him with the leash in your right hand. Reach over him with your left hand and grasp his left foreleg. With your right hand, take his right foreleg and pull his legs forward while you say, "Beau, down." If he tries to get up, lean on his shoulder to encourage him to stay down. It will relax your dog if you stroke his back while he is down. Try to encourage him to stay down for a few seconds as preparation for the Down/Stay.

Heel

The definition of heeling is the dog walking under control at your left heel. Your puppy will learn controlled walking in the puppy kindergarten class, which will eventually lead to heeling. The command is "Beau, heel," and you start off briskly with your left foot. Your leash is

This puppy is being given a donut-shaped chew toy; saying "Take it" while giving the toy is good training for an advanced obedience exercise.

in your right hand and your left hand is holding it about half way down. Your left hand should be able to control the leash and there should be a little slack in it. You want him to walk with you with your leg somewhere between his nose and his shoulder. You need to encourage him to stay with you, not forging (in front of you) or lagging behind you. It is best to keep him on a fairly short lead. Do not allow the lead to become tight. It is far better to give him a little

This pup will soon have his Nylafloss® replaced by a leash so he can strut alongside his owner while seeing the world.

jerk when necessary and remind him to heel. When you come to a halt, be prepared physically to make him sit. It takes practice to become coordinated. There are excellent books on training that you may wish to purchase. Your instructor should be able to recommend one for you.

This dog is obeying the down command given by his owner.

Make "Come" a fun command to obey by getting your puppy's attention and calling him to you for a reward.

Recall

This quite possibly is the most important exercise you will ever teach. It should be a pleasant experience. The puppy may learn to do random recalls while being attached to a long line such as a clothes line. Later the exercise will start with the dog sitting and staying until called. The command is "Beau, come." Let your command be happy. You want your dog to come willingly and faithfully. The recall could save his life if he sneaks out the door. In practicing the recall, let him jump on you or touch you before you reach for him. If he is shy, then kneel down to his level. Reaching for the insecure dog could frighten him, and he may not be willing to come again in the future. Lots of praise and a treat would be in order whenever you do a recall. Under no circumstances should you ever correct your dog when he has come to you. Later in formal obedience your dog will be required to sit in front of you after recalling and then go to heel position.

CONFORMATION

Conformation showing is our oldest dog sport. This type of showing is based on the dog's appearance—that is his structure, movement and attitude. When considering this type of showing, you need to be aware of your breed's standard and be able to evaluate your dog compared to that standard. The breeder of your puppy or other experienced breeders would be good sources for such an evaluation. Puppies can go through lots of changes over a period of time. I always say most puppies start out as promising hopefuls and then after maturing may be disappointing as show candidates. Even so this should not deter them from being excellent pets.

Usually conformation training classes are offered by the local kennel or obedience clubs. These are excellent places for training puppies. The puppy should be able to walk on a lead before entering such a class. Proper ring procedure and technique for posing (stacking) the dog will be demonstrated as well as gaiting the dog. Usually certain patterns are used in the ring such as the triangle or the "L." Conformation class, like the

A lot of work goes into making your dog look good and move well for a judge at a dog show. Here the author judges in Spain.

PKT class, will give your youngster the opportunity to socialize with different breeds of dogs and humans too.

Earning an AKC championship is built on a point system, which is different from Great Britain. To become an AKC Champion of Record the dog must earn 15 points. The number of points earned each time depends upon the number of dogs in competition. The number of points available at each show depends upon the breed, its sex and the location of the show. The United States is divided into ten AKC zones. Each zone has its own set of points. The purpose of the zones is to try to equalize the points available from breed to breed and area to area.The AKC adjusts the point scale annually.

At a dog show, you will asked to gait your dog around the ring according to the judge's instructions.

The number of points that can be won at a show are between one and five. Three-, four- and five-point wins are considered majors. Not only does the dog need 15 points won under three different judges, but those points must include two majors under two different judges. Canada also works on a point system but majors are not required.

Dogs always show before bitches. The classes available to those seeking points are: Puppy (which may be divided into 6 to 9 months and 9 to 12 months); 12 to 18 months; Novice; Bred-by-Exhibitor; American-bred; and Open. The class winners of the same sex of each breed or variety compete against each other for Winners Dog and Winners Bitch. A Reserve Winners Dog and Reserve Winners Bitch are also awarded but do not carry any points unless the Winners win is disallowed by AKC. The Winners Dog and Bitch compete with the specials (those

To the victor go the spoils. This is Ch. Innisfree's Challenger winning a blue ribbon and a book for placing first in the Working Group at a show on Long Island, NY.

dogs that have attained championship) for Best of Breed or Variety, Best of Winners and Best of Opposite Sex. It is possible to pick up an extra point or even a major if the points are higher for the defeated winner than those of Best of Winners. The latter would get the higher total from the defeated winner.

At an all-breed show, each Best of Breed or Variety winner will go on to his respective Group and then the Group winners will compete against each other for Best in Show. There are seven Groups: Sporting, Hounds,

Working, Terriers, Toys, Non-Sporting and Herding. Obviously there are no Groups at speciality shows (those shows that have only one breed or a show such as the American Spaniel Club's Flushing Spaniel Show, which is for all flushing spaniel breeds).

Westminster Kennel Club is our most prestigious show although the entry is limited to 2500. In recent years, entry has been limited to Champions. This show is more formal than the majority of the shows with the judges wearing formal attire and the handlers fashionably dressed. In most instances the quality of the dogs is superb. After all, it is a show of Champions. It is a good show to study the AKC registered breeds and is by far the most exciting—especially since it is televised! WKC is one of the few shows in this country that is still benched. This means the dog must be in his benched

Champion Innisfree's Sno Chief is a multiple award winner in Portugal and Spain, where he lives.

The judge goes over every dog in a class checking for structural correctness before awarding a winner. area during the show hours except when he is being groomed, in the ring, or being exercised.

In England, Crufts is The Kennel Club's own show and is most assuredly the largest dog show in the world. They've been known to have an entry of nearly 20,000, and the show lasts four days. Entry is only gained by qualifying through winning in specified classes at another Championship Show. Westminster is strictly conformation, but Crufts exhibitors and spectators enjoy not only conformation but obedience, agility and a multitude of exhibitions as well. Obedience was admitted in 1957 and agility in 1983.

Junior Showmanship

The Junior Showmanship class is a wonderful way to build self confidence even if there are no aspirations of staying with the dog-show game later in life. Frequently,

Junior Showmanship becomes the background of those who become successful exhibitors/handlers in the future. In some instances it is taken very seriously, and success is measured in terms of wins. The Junior Handler is judged solely on his ability and skill in presenting his dog. The dog's conformation is not to be considered by the judge. Even so the condition and grooming of the dog may be a reflection upon the handler.

Usually the matches and point shows include different classes. The Junior Handler's dog may be entered in a breed or obedience class and even shown by another person in that class. Junior Showmanship classes are usually divided by age and perhaps sex. The age is determined by the handler's age on the day of the show. The classes are:

Novice Junior for those at least ten and under 14 years of age who at time of entry closing have not won three first places in a Novice Class at a licensed or member show.

Novice Senior for those at least 14 and under 18 years of age who at the time of entry closing have not won three first places in a Novice Class at a licensed or member show.

Open Junior for those at least ten and under 14 years of age who at the time of entry closing have won at least three first places in a Novice Junior Showmanship Class at a licensed or member show with competition present.

An overview of the rings set up in Madison Square Garden for the Westminster Kennel Club show in New York.

Open Senior for those at least 14 and under 18 years of age who at time of entry closing have won at least three first places in a Novice Junior Showmanship Class at a licensed or member show with competition present.

Junior Handlers must include their AKC Junior Handler number on each show entry. This needs to be obtained from the AKC.

The markings on this dog's face make him a real eye-catcher.

Conformation shows are held all over the world. This is Italian and International Champion Innisfree's Dallas, who lives in Italy.

The handler is asking her dog to "Down," which is part of the Canine Good Citizen test.

CANINE GOOD CITIZEN

The AKC sponsors a program to encourage dog owners to train their dogs. Local clubs perform the pass/fail tests, and dogs who pass are awarded a Canine Good Citizen Certificate. Proof of vaccination is required at the time of participation. The test includes:

1. Accepting a friendly stranger.
2. Sitting politely for petting.
3. Appearance and grooming.
4. Walking on a loose leash.
5. Walking through a crowd.
6. Sit and down on command/staying in place.
7. Come when called.
8. Reaction to another dog.
9. Reactions to distractions.
10. Supervised separation.

If more effort was made by pet owners to accomplish these exercises, fewer dogs would be cast off to the humane shelter.

OBEDIENCE

Obedience is necessary, without a doubt, but it can also become a wonderful hobby or even an obsession. In my opinion, obedience classes and competition can provide wonderful companionship, not only with your dog but with your classmates or fellow competitors. It is always gratifying to discuss your dog's problems with others who have had similar experiences. The AKC acknowledged Obedience around 1936, and it has changed tremendously even though many of the exercises are basically the same. Today, obedience competition is just that—very competitive. Even so, it is possible for every obedience exhibitor to come home a winner (by earning qualifying scores) even though he/she may not earn a placement in the class.

Teaching "Stay" comes in handy in situations like this, where the dogs' door is open but they're not allowed to come out yet.

Most of the obedience titles are awarded after earning three qualifying scores (legs) in the appropriate class under three different judges. These classes offer a perfect score of 200, which is extremely rare. Each of the class

79

exercises has its own point value. A leg is earned after receiving a score of at least 170 and at least 50 percent of the points available in each exercise. The titles are:

Companion Dog–CD
Companion Dog Excellent–CDX
Utility Dog–UD

After achieving the UD title, you may feel inclined to go after the UDX and/or OTCh. The UDX (Utility Dog Excellent) title went into effect in January 1994. It is not easily attained. The title requires qualifying simultaneously ten times in Open B and Utility B but not necessarily at consecutive shows.

The OTCh (Obedience Trial Champion) is awarded after the dog has earned his UD and then goes on to earn 100 championship points, a first place in Utility, a first place in Open and another first place in either class. The placements must be won under three different judges at all-breed obedience trials. The points are determined by the number of dogs competing in the Open B and Utility

A Nylabone® makes an excellent substitute for a dumbbell because it's something the puppy will want to take and hold in his mouth.

B classes. The OTCh title precedes the dog's name.

Obedience matches (AKC Sanctioned, Fun, and Show and Go) are usually available. Usually they are sponsored by the local obedience

This handsome dog sits alertly waiting for his owner to release him.

clubs. When preparing an obedience dog for a title, you will find matches very helpful. Fun Matches and Show and Go Matches are more lenient in allowing you to make corrections in the ring. I frequently train (correct) in the ring and inform the judge that I would like to do so and to please mark me "exhibition." This means that I will not be eligible for any prize. This type of training is usually very necessary for the Open and Utility Classes. AKC Sanctioned Obedience Matches do not allow corrections in the ring since they must abide by the AKC Obedience Regulations. If you are interested in showing in obedience, then you should contact the AKC for a copy of the Obedience Regulations.

TRACKING

Tracking is officially classified obedience, but I feel it should have its own category. There are three tracking titles available: Tracking Dog (TD), Tracking Dog Excellent (TDX), Variable Surface Tracking (VST).

If your Husky loves to use his nose, tracking could be the sport for you. It's challenging and very rewarding.

If all three tracking titles are obtained, then the dog officially becomes a CT (Champion Tracker). The CT will go in front of the dog's name.

Getting started with tracking requires reading the AKC regulations and a good book on tracking plus finding other tracking enthusiasts. I like to work on the buddy system. That is—we lay tracks for each other so we can practice blind tracks. It is possible to train on your own, but if you are a beginner, it is a lot more entertaining to track with a buddy. Tracking is my favorite dog sport. It's rewarding seeing the dog use his natural ability.

AGILITY

Agility was first introduced by John Varley in England at the Crufts Dog Show, February 1978, but Peter Meanwell, competitor and judge, actually

Trophies are often awarded the first-place finishers of dog sports. Here a row of trophies is set up at a dog show.

developed the idea. It was officially recognized in the early '80s. Agility is extremely popular in England and Canada and growing in popularity in the U.S. The AKC acknowledged agility in August 1994. Dogs must be at least 12 months of age to be entered. It is a fascinating sport that the dog, handler and spectators enjoy to the utmost. Agility is a spectator sport! The dog performs off lead. The handler either runs with his dog or positions himself on the course and directs his dog with verbal and hand signals over a timed course over or through a variety of obstacles including a time out or pause. One of the main drawbacks to agility is finding a place to train. The obstacles take up a lot of space and it is very time consuming to put up and take down courses.

If you train with patience and kindness and keep the training fun, your dog will look forward to working with you on whatever challenge you present him.

The titles earned at AKC agility trials are Novice Agility Dog (NAD), Open Agility Dog (OAD), Agility Dog Excellent (ADX), and Master Agility Excellent (MAX). In order to acquire an agility title, a dog must earn a qualifying score in its respective class on three separate occasions under two different judges. The MAX will be awarded after earning ten qualifying scores in the Agility Excellent Class.

GENERAL INFORMATION

Obedience, tracking and agility allow the purebred dog with an Indefinite Listing Privilege (ILP) number or a limited registration to be exhibited and earn titles. Application must be made to the AKC for an ILP number.

The American Kennel Club publishes a monthly *Events* magazine that is part of the *Gazette*, their official journal for the sport of purebred dogs. The *Events* section lists upcoming shows and the secretary or superintendent for them. The majority of the conformation shows in the U.S. are overseen by licensed superintendents. Generally the entry closing date is approximately two-and-a-half weeks before the actual show. Point shows are fairly expensive, while the match shows cost about one-third of the point show entry fee. The AKC can provide you with a list of superintendents, and you can write and ask to be put on their mailing lists.

A thorough grooming is just one element of preparing your dog for his day at the show.

Obedience trial and tracking test information is available through the AKC. Frequently these events are not superintended, but put on by the host club. Therefore you would make the entry with the event's secretary.

As you have read, there are numerous activities you can share with your dog. Regardless what you do, it does take teamwork. Your dog can only benefit from your attention and training. I hope this chapter has enlightened you and hope, if nothing else, you will attend a show here and there. Perhaps you will start with a puppy kindergarten class, and who knows where it may lead!

HEALTH CARE

Veterinary medicine has become far more sophisticated than what was available to our ancestors. This can be attributed to the increase in household pets and consequently the demand for better care for them. Also human medicine has become far more complex. Today diagnostic testing in veterinary medicine parallels human diagnostics. Because of better technology we can expect our pets to live healthier lives thereby increasing their life spans.

THE FIRST CHECK UP

You will want to take your new puppy/dog in for its first check up within 48 to 72 hours after acquiring it. Many breeders strongly recommend this check up and so do the humane shelters. A puppy/dog can appear healthy but it may have a serious problem that is not apparent to the layman. Most pets have some type of a minor flaw that may never cause a real problem.

Unfortunately if he/she should have a serious problem, you will want to consider the consequences of keeping the pet and the attachments that will be formed, which may be broken prematurely. Keep in mind there are many healthy dogs looking for good homes.

This first check up is a good time to establish yourself with the veterinarian and learn the office policy regarding their hours and how they handle emergencies. Usually the breeder or another conscientious pet owner is a good

By eight to ten weeks of age your puppy should have his first series of shots; however, you should take him to the vet within seventy-two hours of acquiring him.

Puppies need their sleep, and you'll discover they nap easily wherever they tire themselves out.

reference for locating a capable veterinarian. You should be aware that not all veterinarians give the same quality of service. Please do not make your selection on the least expensive clinic, as they may be short changing your pet. There is the possibility that eventually it will cost you more due to improper diagnosis, treatment, etc. If you are selecting a new veterinarian, feel free to ask for a tour of the clinic. You should inquire about making an appointment for a tour since all clinics are working clinics, and therefore may not be available all day for sightseers. You may worry less if you see where your pet will be spending the day if he ever needs to be hospitalized.

THE PHYSICAL EXAM

Your veterinarian will check your pet's overall condition, which includes listening to the heart; checking the respiration; feeling the abdomen, muscles and joints; checking the mouth, which includes the gum color and signs of gum disease along with plaque buildup; checking the ears for signs of an infection or ear mites; examining the eyes; and, last but not least, checking the condition of the skin and coat.

He should ask you questions regarding your pet's eating and elimination habits and invite you to relay your questions. It is a good idea to prepare a list so as not to forget anything. He should discuss the proper diet and the quantity to be fed. If this should differ from your breeder's recommendation, then you should convey to him the breeder's choice and see if he approves. If he

You will want to tell your veterinarian everything about your new puppy the first time you bring him in, including the name of the breeder's kennel where you got him.

Because you will want to travel far and wide with your beautiful Husky, you must vaccinate him against common diseases. recommends changing the diet, then this should be done over a few days so as not to cause a gastrointestinal upset. It is customary to take in a fresh stool sample (just a small amount) for a test for intestinal parasites. It must be fresh, preferably within 12 hours, since the eggs hatch quickly and after hatching will not be observed under the microscope. If your pet isn't obliging then, usually the technician can take one in the clinic.

IMMUNIZATIONS

It is important that you take your puppy/dog's vaccination record with you on your first visit. In case of a puppy, presumably the breeder has seen to the vaccinations up to the time you acquired custody. Veterinarians differ in their vaccination protocol. It is not unusual for your puppy to have received vaccinations for distemper, hepatitis, leptospirosis, parvovirus and parainfluenza every two to three weeks from the age of five or six weeks. Usually this is a combined injection and is typically called the DHLPP. The DHLPP is given through at least 12 to 14 weeks of age, and it is customary to continue with another parvovirus vaccine at 16 to 18 weeks. You may wonder why so many immunizations are necessary. No one knows for sure when the puppy's maternal antibodies are gone, although it is customarily accepted that distemper antibodies are gone by 12 weeks. Usually parvovirus antibodies are gone by 16 to 18 weeks of age. However, it is possible for the maternal antibodies to be gone at a much earlier age or even a later age. Therefore immunizations are started at an early age. The vaccine will not give immunity as long as there are maternal antibodies.

Puppies can pick up germs anywhere and everywhere. He's protected if he's had his shots.

The rabies vaccination is given at three or six months of age depending on your local laws. A vaccine for bordetella (kennel cough) is advisable and can be given anytime from the age of five weeks. The coronavirus is not commonly given unless there is a problem locally. The Lyme vaccine is necessary in endemic areas. Lyme disease has been reported in 47 states.

Distemper

This is virtually an incurable disease. If the dog recovers, he is subject to severe nervous disorders. The virus attacks every

Antibodies to protect against disease are passed on from mother to puppy, but no one knows how long they last, which is why shots are given young.

tissue in the body and resembles a bad cold with a fever. It can cause a runny nose and eyes and cause gastrointestinal disorders, including a poor appetite, vomiting and diarrhea. The virus is carried by raccoons, foxes, wolves, mink and other dogs. Unvaccinated youngsters and senior citizens are very susceptible. This is still a common disease.

Hepatitis

This is a virus that is most serious in very young dogs. It is spread by contact with an infected animal or its stool or urine. The virus affects the liver and kidneys and is characterized by high fever, depression and lack of appetite. Recovered animals may be afflicted with chronic illnesses.

This big dog, with a pink tongue and ears, clear eyes and full coat, is the picture of health.

Leptospirosis

This is a bacterial disease transmitted by contact with the urine of an infected dog, rat or other wildlife. It produces severe symptoms of fever, depression, jaundice and internal bleeding and was fatal before the vaccine was developed. Recovered dogs can be carriers, and the disease can be transmitted from dogs to humans.

Parvovirus

This was first noted in the late 1970s and is still a fatal disease. However, with proper vaccinations, early diagnosis and prompt treatment, it is a manageable disease. It attacks the bone marrow and intestinal tract. The symptoms include depression, loss of appetite, vomiting, diarrhea and collapse. Immediate medical attention is of the essence.

Rabies

This is shed in the saliva and is carried by raccoons, skunks, foxes, other dogs and cats. It attacks nerve tissue, resulting in paralysis and death. Rabies can be transmitted to people and is virtually always fatal. This disease is reappearing in the suburbs.

Dogs that are housed with other dogs are especially susceptible to the bordetella virus that causes kennel cough.

Bordetella (Kennel cough)

The symptoms are coughing, sneezing, hacking and retching accompanied by nasal discharge

usually lasting from a few days to several weeks. There are several disease-producing organisms responsible for this disease. The present vaccines are helpful but do not protect for all the strains. It usually is not life threatening but in some instances it can progress to a serious bronchopneumonia. The disease is highly contagious. The vaccination should be given routinely for dogs that come in contact with other dogs, such as through boarding, training class or visits to the groomer.

Coronavirus

This is usually self limiting and not life threatening. It was first noted in the late '70s about a year before parvovirus. The virus produces a yellow/brown stool and there may be depression, vomiting and diarrhea.

Lyme Disease

This was first diagnosed in the United States in 1976 in Lyme, CT in people who lived in close proximity to the deer tick. Symptoms may include acute lameness, fever, swelling of joints and loss of appetite. Your veterinarian can advise you if you live in an endemic area.

After your puppy has completed his puppy vaccinations, you will continue to booster the DHLPP once a year. It is customary to booster the rabies one year after the first vaccine and then, depending on where you live, it should be boostered every year or every three years. This depends on your local laws. The Lyme and corona vaccines are boostered annually and it is recommended that the bordetella be boostered every six to eight months.

Any puppies or dogs who spend time outdoors should be checked for parasites that cause disease, like ticks and fleas.

ANNUAL VISIT

I would like to impress the importance of the annual check up, which would include the booster vaccinations, check for intestinal parasites and test for heartworm. Today in our very busy world it is rush, rush and see "how much you can get for how little." Unbelievably, some non-veterinary businesses have entered into the vaccination business. More harm than good can come to your dog through improper vaccinations, possibly from inferior vaccines and/or the

An annual visit to the veterinarian will keep potential problems from becoming disasters.

It's a dog's life to nap in a cool dirt hole - just be sure your dog doesn't carry any uninvited guests inside with him.

wrong schedule. More than likely you truly care about your companion dog and over the years you have devoted much time and expense to his well being. Perhaps you are

unaware that a vaccination is not just a vaccination. There is more involved. Please, please follow through with regular physical examinations. It is so important for your veterinarian to know your dog and this is especially true during middle age through the geriatric years. More than likely your older dog will require more than one physical a year. The annual physical is good preventive medicine. Through early diagnosis and subsequent treatment your dog can maintain a longer and better quality of life.

INTESTINAL PARASITES

Hookworms

These are almost microscopic intestinal worms that can cause anemia and therefore serious problems, including death, in young puppies. Hookworms can be transmitted to humans through penetration of the skin. Puppies may be born with them.

You can sometimes tell if your dog is infected with an intestinal parasite because his coat will look dull and he may lack energy. Clearly this beautiful dog has no such problems.

Roundworms

These are spaghetti-like worms that can cause a potbellied appearance and dull coat along with more severe symptoms, such as vomiting, diarrhea and coughing. Puppies acquire these while in the mother's uterus and through lactation. Both hookworms and roundworms may be acquired through ingestion.

This sea-faring Husky may not have to worry about ticks, but flies and heat could be troublesome to him.

Whipworms

These have a three-month life cycle and are not acquired through the dam. They cause intermittent diarrhea usually with mucus. Whipworms are possibly the most difficult worm to eradicate. Their eggs are very resistant to most environmental factors and can last for years until the proper conditions enable them to mature. Whipworms are seldom seen in the stool.

Intestinal parasites are more prevalent in some areas than others. Climate, soil and contamination are big factors contributing to the incidence of intestinal parasites. Eggs are passed in the stool, lay on the ground and then become infective in a certain number of days. Each of the above worms has a different life cycle. Your best chance of becoming and remaining worm-free is to always pooper-scoop your yard. A fenced-in yard keeps stray dogs out, which is certainly helpful.

I would recommend having a fecal examination on your dog twice a year

Whipworms are possibly the most difficult worms to eradicate. They cause intermittent diarrhea, usually with mucus.

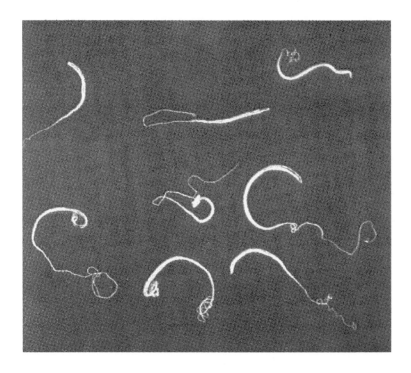

Owners of more than one dog need to be especially diligent about cleaning up their pens and yards because worms can be passed through excrement.

or more often if there is a problem. If your dog has a positive fecal sample, then he will be given the appropriate medication and you will be asked to bring back another stool sample in a certain period of time (depending on the type of worm) and then be rewormed. This process goes on until he has at least two negative samples. The different types of worms require different medications. You will be wasting your money and doing your dog an injustice by buying over-the-counter medication without first consulting your veterinarian.

Fleas are not a concern for Huskies who live in snowy climes, but cold weather has its own dangers that puppies need protection against.

OTHER INTERNAL PARASITES

Coccidiosis and Giardiasis

These protozoal infections usually affect puppies, especially in places where large numbers of puppies are brought together. Older dogs may harbor these infections but do not show signs unless they are stressed. Symptoms include diarrhea, weight loss and lack of appetite. These infections are not always apparent in the fecal examination.

Tapeworms

Seldom apparent on fecal floatation, they are diagnosed frequently as rice-like segments around the dog's anus and the base of the tail. Tapeworms are long, flat and ribbon like, sometimes several feet in length, and made up of many segments about five-eighths of an inch long. The two most common types of tapeworms found in the dog are:

(1) First the larval form of the flea tapeworm parasite must mature in an intermediate host, the flea, before it can become infective. Your dog acquires this by ingesting the flea through licking and chewing.

(2) Rabbits, rodents and certain large game animals serve as intermediate hosts for other species of tapeworms. If your dog should eat one of these infected hosts, then he can acquire tapeworms.

Dirofilaria—adult worms in the heart of a dog. It is possible for a dog to be infected with several hundred worms up to 14 inches long.

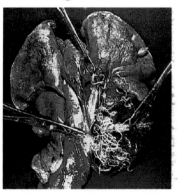

HEARTWORM DISEASE

This is a worm that resides in the heart and adjacent blood vessels of the lung that produces microfilaria, which circulate in the bloodstream. It is possible for a dog to be infected with any number of worms from one to a hundred that can be 6 to 14 inches long. It is a life-threatening disease, expensive to treat and easily prevented. Depending on where you live, your veterinarian may recommend a preventive year-round and either an annual or semiannual blood test. The most common preventive is given once a month.

EXTERNAL PARASITES

Fleas

These pests are not only the dog's worst enemy but also enemy to the owner's pocketbook. Preventing is less expensive than treating, but regardless I think we'd prefer to spend our money elsewhere. I would guess that the majority of our dogs are allergic to the bite of a flea, and in many cases it only takes one flea bite. The protein in the flea's saliva is the culprit. Allergic dogs have a reaction, which usually results in a "hot spot." More than likely such a reaction will involve a trip to the veterinarian for treatment. Yes, prevention is less expensive. Fortunately today there are several good products available.

If there is a flea infestation, no one product is going to correct the problem. Not only will the dog require treatment so will the environment. In general flea collars are not very effective although there is now available an "egg" collar that will kill the eggs on the dog. Dips are the most economical but they are messy. There are some effective shampoos and

Under ideal conditions, fleas can complete their life cycle in three weeks. Courtesy of Fleabusters, Rx for Fleas, Inc., Fort Lauderdale, Florida.

treatments available through pet shops and veterinarians. An oral tablet arrived on the American market in 1995 and was popular in Europe the previous year. It sterilizes the female flea but will

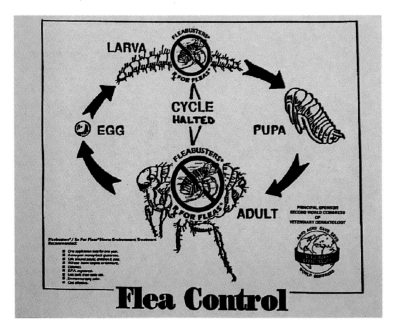

This puppy wants the world to know he's ready for his bath. Washing with a pest-repellent shampoo that's safe for puppies is one part of keeping the environment parasite-free. not kill adult fleas. Therefore the tablet, which is given monthly, will decrease the flea population but is not a "cure-all." Those dogs that suffer from flea-bite allergy will still be subjected to the bite of the flea. Another popular parasiticide is permethrin, which is applied to the back of the dog in one or two places depending on the dog's weight. This product works as a repellent causing the flea to get "hot feet" and jump off. Do not confuse this product with some of the organophosphates that are also applied to the dog's back.

Some products are not usable on young puppies. Treating fleas should be done under your veterinarian's guidance. Frequently it is necessary to combine products and the layman does not have the knowledge regarding possible toxicities. It is hard to believe but there are a few dogs that do have a natural resistance to fleas. Nevertheless it would be wise to treat all pets at the same time. Don't forget your cats. Cats just love to prowl the neighborhood and consequently return with unwanted guests.

Adult fleas live on the dog but their eggs drop off the dog into the environment. There they go through four larval stages before reaching adulthood, and thereby are able to jump back on the poor unsuspecting dog. The cycle resumes and takes between 21 to 28 days under ideal conditions. There are environmental products available that will kill both the adult fleas and the larvae.

Ticks

Ticks carry Rocky Mountain Spotted Fever, Lyme disease and can cause tick paralysis. They should be removed with tweezers, trying to pull out the head. The jaws carry disease. There is a tick preventive collar that does an excellent job. The ticks automatically back out on those dogs wearing collars.

This champion is kept in top condition. He is American and Canadian Ch. Innisfree Fire and Frost, CGC, rated #1 Siberian in 1992 and '93.

If you notice your puppy itching excessively or losing hair, he may have a type of mange.

Sarcoptic Mange

This is a mite that is difficult to find on skin scrapings. The pinnal reflex is a good indicator of this disease. Rub the ends of the pinna (ear) together and the dog will start scratching with his foot. Sarcoptes are highly contagious to other dogs and to humans although they do not live long on humans. They cause intense itching.

Demodectic Mange

This is a mite that is passed from the dam to her puppies. It affects youngsters age three to ten months. Diagnosis is confirmed by skin scraping. Small areas of alopecia around the eyes, lips and/or forelegs become visible. There is little itching unless there is a secondary bacterial infection. Some breeds are afflicted more than others.

Cheyletiella

This causes intense itching and is diagnosed by skin scraping. It lives in the outer layers of the skin of dogs, cats, rabbits and humans. Yellow-gray scales may be found on the back and the rump, top of the head and the nose.

TO BREED OR NOT TO BREED

More than likely your breeder has requested that you have your puppy neutered or spayed. Your breeder's request is based on what is healthiest for your dog and what is most beneficial for your breed. Experienced and conscientious breeders devote many years into developing a bloodline. In order to do this, he makes every effort to plan each breeding in regard to conformation, temperament and health. This type of breeder does his best to perform the necessary testing (i.e., OFA, CERF, testing for inherited blood disorders, thyroid, etc.). Testing is expensive and sometimes very disheartening when a favorite dog doesn't pass his health

The sight of a mother and her puppies is a sweet one, but only those with a commitment to bettering the breed and properly raising every puppy should consider breeding their dog.

tests. The health history pertains not only to the breeding stock but to the immediate ancestors. Reputable breeders do not want their offspring to be bred indiscriminately. Therefore you may be asked to neuter or spay your puppy. Of course there is always the exception, and your breeder may agree to let you breed your dog under his direct supervision. This is an important concept. More and more effort is being made to breed healthier dogs.

Spay/Neuter

There are numerous benefits of performing this surgery at six months of age. Unspayed females are subject to mammary and ovarian cancer. In order to prevent mammary cancer she must be spayed prior to her first heat cycle. Later in life, an unspayed female may develop a pyometra (an infected uterus), which is definitely life threatening.

Spaying is performed under a general anesthetic and is easy on the young dog. As you might expect it is

Laboratory tests are studied by highly trained veterinary technicians. Most tests are performed right in your veterinarian's office and results are usually available the same day.

a little harder on the older dog, but that is no reason to deny her the surgery. The surgery removes the ovaries and uterus. It is important to remove all the ovarian tissue. If some is left behind, she could remain attractive to males. In order to view the ovaries, a reasonably long incision is necessary. An ovariohysterectomy is considered major surgery.

Neutering the male at a young age will inhibit some characteristic male behavior that owners frown upon. I have found my boys will not hike their legs and mark territory if they are neutered at six months of age. Also neutering at a young age has hormonal benefits, lessening the chance of hormonal aggressiveness.

Surgery involves removing the testicles but leaving the scrotum. If there should be a retained testicle, then he definitely needs to be neutered before the age of two or three years. Retained testicles can develop into cancer. Unneutered males are at risk for testicular cancer, perineal fistulas, perianal tumors and fistulas and prostatic disease.

Intact males and females are prone to housebreaking accidents. Females urinate frequently before, during and after heat cycles, and males tend to mark territory if there is a female in heat. Males may show the same behavior if there is a visiting dog or guests.

Surgery involves a sterile operating procedure equivalent to human surgery. The incision site is shaved, surgically scrubbed and draped. The veterinarian wears a sterile

Siberians sold as pets should be neutered from an early age to make them easier to live with and protect them against reproductive diseases later in life.

Neutering or spaying your male or female will not affect his or her ability to do whatever you want with your pet, including race.

surgical gown, cap, mask and gloves. Anesthesia should be monitored by a registered technician. It is customary for the veterinarian to recommend a pre-anesthetic blood screening, looking for metabolic problems and a ECG rhythm strip to check for normal heart function. Today anesthetics are equal to human anesthetics, which enables your dog to walk out of the clinic the same day as surgery.

Some folks worry about their dog gaining weight after being neutered or spayed. This is usually not the case. It is true that some dogs may be less active so they could develop a problem, but my own dogs are just as active as they were before surgery. I have a hard time keeping weight on them. However, if your dog should begin to gain, then you need to decrease his food and see to it that he gets a little more exercise.

Medical Problems

Anal Sacs

These are small sacs on either side of the rectum that can cause the dog discomfort when they are full. They should empty when the dog has a bowel movement. Symptoms of inflammation or impaction are excessive licking under the tail and/or a bloody or sticky discharge from the anal area. Breeders like myself recommend emptying the sacs on a regular schedule when bathing the dog. Many veterinarians prefer this isn't done unless there are symptoms. You can express the sacs by squeezing the two sacs (at the five and seven o'clock positions) in and up toward the anus. Take precautions not to get in the way of the foul-smelling fluid that is expressed. Some dogs object to this procedure so it would be wise to have someone hold the head. Scooting is caused by anal-sac irritation and not worms.

Colitis

The stool may be frank blood or blood tinged and is the result of inflammation of the colon. Colitis, sometimes intermittent, can be the result of stress, undiagnosed whipworms, or perhaps idiopathic (no explainable reason). I have had several dogs prone to this disorder. They felt fine and were willing to eat but would have intermittent bloody stools. If this in an ongoing problem, you should probably feed a diet higher in fiber. Seek professional help if your dog feels poorly and/or the condition persists.

Conjunctivitis

Many breeds are prone to this problem. The conjunctiva is the pink tissue that lines the inner surface of the eyeball except the clear, transparent cornea. Irritating substances such as bacteria, foreign matter or chemicals can cause it to become reddened and swollen. It is important to keep any hair trimmed from around the eyes. Long hair stays damp and aggravates the problem. Keep the eyes cleaned with warm water and wipe away any matter that has accumulated in the corner of the eyes. If the condition persists, you should see your veterinarian. This problem goes hand in hand with keratoconjunctivitis sicca.

Ear Infection

Otitis externa is an inflammation of the external ear canal that begins at the outside opening of the ear and extends inward to the eardrum. Dogs with pendulous ears are prone to this disease, but isn't it interesting that breeds with upright ears also have a high incidence of problems?

Any number of things can cause the inner lining of your puppy's eyes to become irritated or infected.

Allergies, food and inhalent, along with hormonal problems, such as hypothyroidism, are major contributors to the disease. For those dogs which have recurring problems you need to investigate the underlying cause if you hope to cure them.

I recommend that you are careful never to get water into the ears. Water provides a great medium for bacteria to grow. If your dog swims or you inadvertently get water into his ears, then use a drying agent. An at-home preparation would be to use equal parts of three-percent hydrogen peroxide and 70-percent rubbing alcohol. Another preparation is equal parts of white vinegar and water. Your veterinarian alternatively can provide a suitable product. When cleaning the ears, be careful of using cotton tip applicators since they make it easy to pack debris down into the canal. Only clean what you can see.

Because Huskies have prick ears that stand up when they're full grown, they are less prone to ear infections.

If your dog has an ongoing infection, don't be surprised if your veterinarian recommends sedating him and flushing his ears with a bulb syringe. Sometimes this needs to be done a few times to get the ear clean. The ear must be clean so that medication can come in contact with the canal. Be prepared to return for rechecks until the infection is gone. This may involve more flushings if the ears are very bad.

A thorough face-cleaning should be part of your regular grooming routine.

For chronic or recurring cases, your veterinarian may recommend thyroid testing, etc., and a hypoallergenic diet for a trial period of 10 to 12 weeks. Depending on your dog, it may be a good idea to see a dermatologist. Ears shouldn't be taken lightly. If the condition gets out of hand, then surgery may be necessary. Please ask your veterinarian to explain proper ear maintenance for your dog.

Flea Bite Allergy

This is the result of a hypersensitivity to the bite of a flea and its saliva. It only takes one bite to cause the dog to chew or scratch himself raw. Your dog may need medical attention to ease his discomfort. You need to clip the hair around the "hot spot" and wash it with a mild soap and water and you may need to do this daily if the area weeps. Apply an antibiotic anti-inflammatory product. Hot spots can occur from other trauma, such as grooming.

Interdigital Cysts

Check for these on your dog's feet if he shows signs of lameness. They are frequently associated with staph infections and can be quite painful. A home remedy is to soak the infected foot in a solution of a half teaspoon of bleach in a couple of quarts of water. Do this two to three times a day for a couple of days. Check with your veterinarian for an alternative remedy; antibiotics usually work well. If there is a recurring problem, surgery may be required.

Lameness

It may only be an interdigital cyst or it could be

Lameness is something you can spot right away if you spend time watching your dog. Don't risk it getting worse; consult with your veterinarian if your dog is off his stride.

a mat between the toes, especially if your dog licks his feet. Sometimes it is hard to determine which leg is affected. If he is holding up his leg, then you need to see your veterinarian.

The pink tummy on this sleeping puppy is a sign of good health.

Skin

Frequently poor skin is the result of an allergy to fleas, an inhalant allergy or food allergy. These types of problems usually result in a staph dermatitis. Dogs with food allergy usually show signs of severe itching and scratching. However, I have had some dogs with food allergies that never once itched. Their only symptom was swelling of the ears with no ear infection. Food allergy may result in recurrent bacterial skin and ear infections. Your veterinarian or dermatologist will recommend a good restricted diet. It is not wise for you to hit and miss with different dog foods. Many of the diets offered over the counter are not the hypoallergenic diet you are led to believe. Dogs acquire allergies through exposure.

Inhalant allergies result in atopy, which causes licking of the feet, scratching the body and rubbing the muzzle. It may be seasonable. Your veterinarian or dermatologist can perform intradermal testing for inhalant allergies. If your dog should test positive, then a vaccine may be prepared. The results are very satisfying.

Tonsillitis

Usually young dogs have a higher incidence of this problem than the older ones. The older dogs have built up resistance. It is very contagious. Sometimes it is difficult to determine if it is tonsillitis or kennel cough since the symptoms are similar. Symptoms include fever, poor eating, swallowing with difficulty and retching up a white, frothy mucus.

DENTAL CARE for Your Dog's Life

So you've got a new puppy! You also have a new set of puppy teeth in your household. Anyone who has ever raised a puppy is abundantly aware of these new teeth. Your puppy will chew anything it can reach, chase your shoelaces, and play "tear the rag" with any piece of clothing it can find. When puppies are newly born, they have no teeth. At about four weeks of age, puppies of most breeds begin to develop their deciduous or baby teeth. They begin eating semi-solid food, fighting and biting with their litter mates,

To keep your dog's teeth clean and healthy requires regular attention.

and learning discipline from their mother. As their new teeth come in, they inflict more pain on their mother's breasts, so her feeding sessions become less frequent and shorter. By six or eight weeks, the mother will start growling to warn her pups when they are fighting too roughly or hurting her as they nurse too much with their new teeth.

Puppies need to chew. It is a necessary part of their physical and mental development. They develop muscles and necessary life skills as they drag objects around, fight over possession, and vocalize alerts and warnings. Puppies chew on things to explore their world. They are using their sense of taste to determine what is food and what is not. How else can they tell an

Nylabones® help promote tooth and gum health by giving your dog something safe and strong to chew.

electrical cord from a lizard? At about four months of age, most puppies begin shedding their baby teeth. Often these teeth need some help to come out and make way for the permanent teeth. The incisors (front teeth) will be replaced first. Then, the adult canine or fang teeth erupt. When the baby tooth is not shed before the permanent tooth comes in, veterinarians call it a retained deciduous tooth. This condition will often cause gum infections by trapping hair and debris between the permanent tooth and the retained baby tooth. Nylafloss® is an excellent device for puppies to use. They can toss it, drag it, and chew on the many surfaces it presents. The baby teeth can catch in the nylon material, aiding in their removal. Puppies that have adequate chew toys will have less destructive behavior, develop more physically, and have less chance of retained deciduous teeth.

During the first year, your dog should be seen by your veterinarian at regular intervals. Your veterinarian will let you know when to bring in your puppy for vaccinations and parasite examinations. At each visit, your veterinarian should inspect the lips, teeth, and mouth as part of a complete physical examination. You should take some part in the maintenance of your dog's oral health. You should examine your dog's mouth weekly throughout his first year to make sure there are no sores, foreign objects, tooth problems, etc. If your dog drools excessively, shakes its head, or has bad breath, consult your veterinarian. By the time your dog is six months old, the permanent teeth are all in and plaque can start to accumulate on

Ch. Innisfree's Fire and Frost "talks" to his puppies about good oral hygiene: "Don't forget to Nylafloss®!"

118

This puppy will never be the victim of doggy breath. He gets right into the sink to get his choppers washed.

the tooth surfaces. This is when your dog needs to develop good dental-care habits to prevent calculus build-up on its teeth. Brushing is best. That is a fact that cannot be denied. However, some dogs do not like their teeth brushed regularly, or you may not be able to accomplish the task. In that case, you should consider a product that will help prevent plaque and calculus build-up.

The Plaque Attackers® and Galileo Bone® are other excellent choices for the first three years of a dog's life. Their shapes make them interesting for the dog. As the dog chews on them, the solid polyurethane massages the gums which improves the blood circulation to the periodontal tissues. Projections on the chew devices increase the surface and are in contact with the tooth for more efficient cleaning. The unique shape and consistency prevent your dog from exerting excessive force on his own teeth or from breaking off pieces of the bone. If your dog is an aggressive chewer or weighs more than 55 pounds (25 kg), you should consider giving him a Nylabone®, the most durable chew product on the market.

The Gumabones ®, made by Nylabone®, is constructed of strong polyurethane, which is softer than nylon. Less powerful chewers prefer the Gumabones® to the Nylabones®. A super option for your dog is the Hercules Bone®, a uniquely shaped bone named after the great Olympian for its exception strength. Like all Nylabone® products, they are specially scented to make them attractive to your dog. Ask your veterinarian about these bones and he will validate the good doctor's prescription: Nylabones® not only give your dog a good chewing workout but also help to save your dog's teeth (and even his life, as it protects him from possible fatal periodontal diseases).

By the time dogs are four years old, 75% of them have periodontal disease. It is the most common infection in dogs. Yearly examinations by your veterinarian are essential to maintaining your dog's good health. If your veterinarian detects periodontal disease, he or she may

The special nubs on this Nylabone® rub against a dog's teeth while he chews, scraping off plaque. That's why it's called a Plaque-Attacker.®

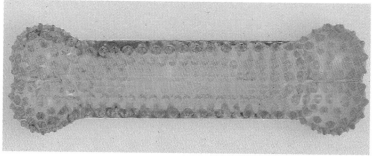

recommend a prophylactic cleaning. To do a thorough cleaning, it will be necessary to put your dog under anesthesia. With modern gas anesthetics and monitoring equipment, the procedure is pretty safe. Your veterinarian will scale the teeth with an ultrasound scaler or hand instrument. This removes the calculus from the teeth. If there are calculus deposits

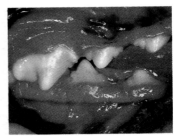

You can see that this dog's teeth have little plaque and tartar build up and that the gums look pink and healthy.

below the gum line, the veterinarian will plane the roots to make them smooth. After all of the calculus has been removed, the teeth are polished with pumice in a polishing cup. If any medical or surgical treatment is needed, it is done at this time. The final step would be

These dogs enjoy their rawhide donuts while their friend looks for one.

fluoride treatment and your follow-up treatment at home. If the periodontal disease is

advanced, the veterinarian may prescribe a medicated mouth rinse or antibiotics for use at home. Make sure your dog has safe, clean and attractive chew toys and treats. Chooz® treats are another way of using a consumable treat to help keep your dog's teeth clean.

Rawhide is the most popular of all materials for a dog to chew. This has never been good news to dog owners, because rawhide is inherently very dangerous for dogs. Thousands of dogs have died from rawhide, having swallowed the hide after it has become soft and mushy, only to cause stomach and intestinal blockage. A new rawhide product on the market has finally solved the problem of rawhide: molded Roar-Hide® from Nylabone®. These are composed of processed, cut up, and melted American rawhide injected into your dog's favorite shape: a dog bone. These dog-safe devices smell and taste like rawhide but don't break up. The ridges on the bones help to fight tartar build-up on the teeth and they last ten times longer than the usual rawhide chews.

As your dog ages, professional examination and cleaning should become more frequent. The mouth should be inspected at least once a year. Your veterinarian may recommend visits every six months. In the geriatric patient, organs such as the heart, liver, and

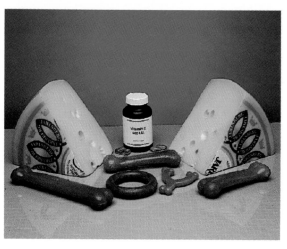

Chew toys don't have to be boring to your dog. Nylabones® come in all shapes and flavors.

This puppy is doing well by his teeth by gnawing on his Nylafloss® and well by his owner by not gnawing on furniture.

kidneys do not function as well as when they were young. Your veterinarian will probably want to test these organs' functions prior to using general anesthesia for dental cleaning. If your dog is a good chewer and you work closely with your veterinarian, your dog can keep all of its teeth all of its life. However, as your dog ages, his sense of smell, sight, and taste will diminish. He may not have the desire to chase, trap or chew his toys. He will also not have the energy to chew for long periods, as arthritis and periodontal disease make chewing painful. This will leave you with more responsibility for keeping his teeth clean and healthy. The dog that would not let you brush his teeth at one year of age, may let you brush his teeth now that he is ten years old.

If you train your dog with good chewing habits as a puppy, he will have healthier teeth throughout his life.

TRAVELING with Your Dog

The earlier you start traveling with your new puppy or dog, the better. He needs to become accustomed to traveling. However, some dogs are nervous riders and become carsick easily. It is helpful if he starts with an empty stomach. Do not despair, as it will go better if you continue taking him with you on short fun rides. How would you feel if every time you rode in the car you stopped at the doctor's for an injection? You would soon dread that nasty car. Older dogs that tend to get carsick may have more of a problem adjusting to traveling. Those dogs that are having a serious problem may benefit from some medication prescribed by the veterinarian.

Siberians are happy to accompany their owners on their travels. This dog poses with the author's daughter and some friends.

Have Husky, will travel! The Briggs family packs Dakota into the pickup for a ride.

Do give your dog a chance to relieve himself before getting into the car. It is a good idea to be prepared for a clean up with a leash, paper towels, bag and terry cloth towel.

The safest place for your dog is in a fiberglass crate, although close confinement can promote carsickness in some dogs. If your dog is nervous you can try letting him ride on the seat next to you or in someone's lap.

An alternative to the crate would be to use a car harness made for dogs and/or a safety strap attached to the harness or collar. Whatever you do, do not let your dog ride in the back of a pickup truck unless he is securely tied on a very short lead. I've seen trucks stop quickly and, even though the dog was tied, it fell out and was dragged.

I do occasionally let my dogs ride loose with me because I really enjoy their companionship, but in all honesty they are safer in their crates. I have a friend whose van rolled in an accident but his dogs, in their fiberglass crates, were not injured nor did they escape. Another advantage of the crate is that it is a safe place to leave him if you need to run into the store. Otherwise you wouldn't be able to leave the windows down. Keep in mind that while many dogs are overly protective in their crates, this may not be enough to deter dognappers. In some states it is against the law to leave a dog in the car unattended.

Never leave a dog loose in the car wearing a collar and leash. I have known more than one dog that has killed himself by hanging. Do not let him put his head out an open window. Foreign debris can be blown into his eyes. When leaving your dog unattended in a car, consider the temperature. It can take less than five minutes to reach temperatures over 100 degrees Fahrenheit.

TRIPS

Perhaps you are taking a trip. Give consideration to what is best for your dog— traveling with you or

The safest way for your dog to travel in a vehicle with you is in a crate—another advantage of crate-training.

There are many ways to travel, and this may be one of the most enjoyable for man and dog. boarding. When traveling by car, van or motor home, you need to think ahead about locking your vehicle. In all probability you have many valuables in the car and do not wish to leave it unlocked. Perhaps most valuable and not replaceable is your dog. Give thought to securing your vehicle and providing adequate ventilation for him. Another consideration for you when traveling with your dog is medical problems that may arise and little inconveniences, such as exposure to external parasites. Some areas of the country are quite flea infested. You may want to carry flea spray with you. This is even a good idea when staying in motels. Quite possibly you are not the only occupant of the room.

Unbelievably many motels and even hotels do allow canine guests, even some very first-class ones. Gaines Pet Foods Corporation publishes *Touring With Towser*, a directory of domestic hotels and motels that accommodate guests with dogs. Their address is Gaines TWT, PO Box 5700, Kankakee, IL, 60902. I would recommend you call ahead to any motel that you may be considering and see if they accept pets. Sometimes it is necessary to pay a deposit against room damage. Of course you are more likely to gain accommodations for a small dog than a large dog. Also the management feels reassured when you mention that your dog will be crated. Since my dogs tend to bark when I leave the room, I leave the TV on nearly full blast to deaden the noises outside that tend to encourage my dogs to bark. If you do travel with your dog, take along plenty of baggies so that you can clean up after him. When we all do our share in cleaning up, we make it possible for motels to continue accepting our pets. As a matter of fact, you should practice cleaning up everywhere you take your dog.

Depending on where your are traveling, you may need an up-to-date health certificate issued by your veterinarian. It is good policy to take along your dog's medical information, which would include the name, address and phone number of your veterinarian, vaccination record, rabies certificate, and any medication he is taking.

A delicious Carrot Bone™ from Nylabone® is the perfect take-along for a traveling dog. It'll keep him occupied for hours.

AIR TRAVEL

When traveling by air, you need to contact the airlines to check their policy. Usually you have to make arrangements up to a couple of weeks in advance for traveling with your dog. The airlines require your dog to travel in an airline approved fiberglass crate. Usually these can be purchased through the airlines but they are also readily available in most pet-supply stores.

If you love your dog so much you can't be parted from him for even a day, study up on the best ways to travel together.

Many of the country's top-winning dogs, like Asian and American Ch. Innisfree's Ice-T, safely travel from dog show to dog show by plane.

If your dog is not accustomed to a crate, then it is a good idea to get him acclimated to it before your trip. The day of the actual trip you

should withhold water about one hour ahead of departure and no food for about 12 hours. The airlines generally have temperature restrictions, which do not allow pets to travel if it is either too cold or too hot. Frequently these restrictions are based on the temperatures at the departure and arrival airports. It's best to inquire about a health certificate. These usually need to be issued within ten days of departure. You should arrange for non-stop, direct flights and if a commuter plane should be involved, check to see if it will carry dogs. Some don't. The Humane Society of the United States has put together a tip sheet for airline traveling. You can receive a copy by sending a self-addressed stamped envelope to:

These puppies stand on their hind legs to get a better view of their owner saying goodbye.

The Humane Society of the US
Tip Sheet
2100 L Street NW
Washington, DC 20037.

Regulations differ for traveling outside of the country and are sometimes changed without notice. Well in advance you need to write or call the

appropriate consulate or agricultural department for instructions. Some countries have lengthy quarantines (six months), and countries differ in their rabies vaccination requirements. For instance, it may have to be given at least 30 days ahead of your departure.

Feed your dog several hours before you plan to travel so the food is digested and you won't have to worry about him getting sick en route.

Do make sure your dog is wearing proper identification. You never know when you might be in an accident and separated from your dog. Or your dog could be frightened and somehow manage to escape and run away. When I travel, my dogs wear collars with engraved nameplates with my name, phone number and city.

Another suggestion would be to carry in-case-of-emergency instructions. These would include the address and phone number of a relative or friend, your veterinarian's name, address and phone number, and your dog's medical information.

Boarding Kennels

Perhaps you have decided that you need to board your dog. Your veterinarian can recommend a good boarding facility or possibly a pet sitter that will come to your house. It is customary for the boarding kennel to ask for proof of vaccination for the DHLPP, rabies and bordetella vaccine. The bordetella should have been given within six months of boarding. This is for your protection. If they do not ask for this proof I would not board at their kennel. Ask about flea control. Those dogs that suffer flea-bite allergy can get in trouble at a boarding kennel. Unfortunately boarding kennels are limited on how much they are able to do.

Many travelers keep their dogs in kennels while they're away. Your veterinarian can probably recommend a clean kennel where dogs are well taken care of.

You may want to hire a professional pet sitter to watch your pup while you're away. Don't worry, he'll still miss you while you're gone.

For more information on pet sitting, contact NAPPS: National Association of Professional Pet Sitters 1200 G Street, NW Suite 760 Washington, DC 20005.

Our clinic has technicians that pet sit and technicians that board clinic patients in their homes. This may be an alternative for you. Ask your veterinarian if they have an employee that can help you. There is a definite advantage of having a technician care for your dog, especially if your dog is on medication or is a senior citizen.

You can write for a copy of *Traveling With Your Pet* from ASPCA, Education Department, 441 E. 92nd Street, New York, NY 10128.

BEHAVIOR and Canine Communication

Studies of the human/animal bond point out the importance of the unique relationships that exist between people and their pets. Those of us who share our lives with pets understand the special part they play through companionship, service and protection. Senior citizens show more concern for their own eating habits when they have the responsibility of feeding a dog. Seeing that their dog is routinely exercised encourages the owner to think of schedules that otherwise may seem unimportant to the senior citizen. The older owner may be arthritic and feeling poorly but with responsibility *Your canine companion will constantly surprise you with his behavior.*

for his dog he has a reason to get up and get moving. It is a big plus if his dog is an attention seeker who will demand such from his owner.

Over the last couple of decades, it has been shown that pets relieve the stress of those who lead busy lives. Owning a pet has been known to lessen the occurrence of heart attack and stroke.

Many single folks thrive on the companionship of a dog. Lifestyles are very different from a long time ago, and today more individuals seek the single life. However, they receive fulfillment from owning a dog.

Most likely the majority of our dogs live in family environments. The companionship they provide is well worth the effort involved. In my opinion, every child should have the opportunity to have a family dog. Dogs teach responsibility through understanding their care, feelings and even respecting their life cycles. Frequently those children who have not been exposed to dogs grow up afraid of dogs, which isn't good. Dogs sense timidity and some will take advantage of the situation.

Man and dog have been friends for ages because the relationship is good for both of them.

Today more dogs are serving as service dogs. Since the origination of the Seeing Eye dogs years ago, we now have trained hearing dogs. Also dogs are trained to provide service for the handicapped and are able to perform many different tasks for their owners. Search and Rescue dogs, with their handlers, are sent throughout the world to assist in recovery of disaster victims. They are life savers.

Therapy dogs are very popular with nursing homes, and some hospitals even allow them to visit. The inhabitants truly look forward to their visits. I have taken a couple of my dogs visiting and left in tears when I saw the response of the patients. They wanted and were allowed to have my dogs in their beds to hold and love.

Nationally there is a Pet Awareness Week to educate students and others about the value and basic care of our pets. Many countries take an even greater interest in their pets than Americans do. In those countries the pets are allowed to accompany their owners into restaurants and shops, etc. In the U.S. this freedom is only available to our service dogs. Even so we think very highly of the human/animal bond.

CANINE BEHAVIOR

Canine behavior problems are the number-one reason for pet owners to dispose of their dogs, either through new homes, humane shelters or euthanasia. Unfortunately there are too many owners who are unwilling to devote the necessary time to properly train their dogs. On the other hand, there are those who not only are concerned about inherited health problems but are also aware of the dog's mental stability.

You may realize that a breed and his group relatives (i.e., sporting, hounds, etc.) show tendencies to behavioral characteristics. An experienced breeder can acquaint you with his breed's personality. Unfortunately many breeds are labeled with poor

Breed types do have certain characteristics. It's a fact: Huskies love snow.

136

Many people don't realize what mischief-makers dogs can be until they get one. Behavior problems are the number-one reason people give up their dogs.

temperaments when actually the breed as a whole is not affected but only a small percentage of individuals within the breed.

If the breed in question is very popular, then of course there may be a higher number of unstable dogs. Do not label a breed good or bad. I know of absolutely awful-tempered dogs within one of our most popular, lovable breeds.

Inheritance and environment contribute to the dog's behavior. Some naïve people suggest inbreeding as the cause of bad temperaments. Inbreeding only results in poor behavior if the ancestors carry the trait. If there are excellent temperaments behind the dogs, then inbreeding will promote good temperaments in the offspring. Did you ever consider that inbreeding is what sets the characteristics of a breed? A purebred dog is the end result of inbreeding. This does not spare the mixed-breed dog from the same problems. Mixed-breed dogs frequently are the offspring of purebred dogs.

When planning a breeding, I like to observe the potential stud and his offspring in the show ring. If I see unruly behavior, I try to look into it further. I want to know if it is genetic or environmental, due to the lack of training and socialization. A good breeder will avoid breeding mentally unsound dogs.

Not too many decades ago most of our dogs led a different lifestyle than what is prevalent today. Usually mom stayed home so the dog had human companionship and someone to discipline it if needed. Not much was expected from the dog. Today's mom works and everyone's life is at a much faster pace.

The dog may have to adjust to being a "weekend" dog. The family is gone all day during the week, and the dog is left to his own devices for entertainment. Some dogs sleep all day waiting for their family to come home and others become wigwam wreckers if given the opportunity. Crates do ensure the safety of the dog and the house. However, he could become a physical and emotional cripple if he doesn't get enough exercise and attention. We still appreciate and want the companionship of our dogs although we expect more from them. In many cases we tend to forget dogs are just that—*dogs* not human beings.

The puppy on the left lets his littermate know he's boss by giving him a little nip on the muzzle.

I own several dogs who are left crated during the day but I do try to make time for them in the evenings and on the weekends. Also we try to do something together before I leave for work. Maybe it helps them to have the companionship of other dogs. They accept their crates as their personal

Like people, puppies go through different developmental stages, which is why it's important to get a puppy from someone who spent quality time with him from birth on.

"houses" and seem to be content with their routine and thrive on trying their best to please me.

Socializing and Training

Many prospective puppy buyers lack experience regarding the proper socialization and training needed to develop the type of pet we all desire. In the first 18 months, training does take some work. Trust me, it is easier to start proper training before there is a problem that needs to be corrected.

The initial work begins with the breeder. The breeder should start socializing the puppy at five to six weeks of age and cannot let up. Human socializing is critical up through 12 weeks of age and likewise important during the following months. The litter should be left together during the first few weeks but it is necessary to separate them by ten weeks of age. Leaving them together after that time will increase competition for litter dominance. If puppies are not socialized with people by 12 weeks of age, they will be timid in later life.

The eight- to ten-week age period is a fearful time for puppies. They need to be handled very gently around

This puppy sure looks pretty, but he's going to need at least one basic training class to teach him how to be a polite pet.

children and adults. There should be no harsh discipline during this time. Starting at 14 weeks of age, the puppy begins the juvenile period, which ends when he reaches sexual maturity around six to 14 months of age. During the juvenile period he needs to be introduced to strangers (adults, children and other dogs) on the home property. At sexual maturity he will begin to bark at strangers and become more protective. Males start to lift their legs to urinate but if you desire you can inhibit this behavior by walking your boy on leash away from trees, shrubs, fences, etc.

Perhaps you are thinking about an older puppy. You need to inquire about the puppy's social experience. If he has lived in a kennel, he may have a hard time adjusting to people and environmental stimuli. Assuming he has had a good social upbringing, there are advantages to an older puppy.

Training includes puppy kindergarten and a minimum of one to two basic training classes. During these classes you will learn how to dominate your youngster. This is especially important if you own a large breed of dog. It is somewhat harder, if not nearly impossible, for some owners to be the Alpha figure when their dog towers over them. You will be taught how to properly restrain your dog. This concept is important. Again it puts you in the Alpha position. All dogs need to be restrained many times during their lives. Believe it or not, some of our worst offenders are the eight-week-old puppies that are brought to our clinic. They need to be gently restrained for a nail trim but the way they carry on you would think we were killing them. In comparison, their vaccination is a "piece of cake." When we ask dogs to do something that is not agreeable to them, then their worst comes out. Life will be easier for your dog if you expose him at a young age to the necessities of life—proper behavior and restraint.

What do you think this puppy's eyes and body language say? If only he could talk!

UNDERSTANDING THE DOG'S LANGUAGE

Most authorities agree that the dog is a descendent of the wolf. The dog and wolf have similar traits. For instance both are pack oriented and prefer not to be isolated for long periods of time. Another characteristic is that the dog, like the wolf, looks to the leader—Alpha—for direction. Both the wolf and the dog communicate through body language, not only within their pack but with outsiders.

Every pack has an Alpha figure. The dog looks to you, or should look to you, to be that leader. If your dog doesn't receive the proper training and guidance, he very well may replace you as Alpha. This would be a serious problem and is certainly a disservice to your dog.

Eye contact is one way the Alpha wolf keeps order within his pack. You are Alpha so you must establish eye contact with your puppy. Obviously your puppy will have to look at you. Practice eye contact even if you need to hold his head for five to ten seconds at a time. You can give him a treat as a reward. Make sure your eye contact is gentle and not threatening. Later, if he has been naughty, it is permissible to give him a long, penetrating look. I caution you there are some older dogs that never learned eye contact as puppies and cannot accept eye contact. You should avoid eye contact with these dogs since they feel threatened and will retaliate as such.

Body Language

The play bow, when the forequarters are down and the hindquarters are elevated, is an invitation to play. Puppies play fight, which helps them learn the acceptable limits of biting. This is necessary for later in their lives. Nevertheless, an owner may be falsely reassured by the playful nature of his dog's aggression. Playful aggression toward another dog or human may be an indication of serious aggression in the future. Owners should never play fight or play tug-of-war with any dog that is inclined to be dominant.

You can tell these two dogs want to play with each other by the way their tails are wagging and they're nudging and looking at each other.

Signs of submission are:
    1. Avoids eye contact.
    2. Active submission—
the dog crouches down,
ears back and the tail is
lowered.
    3. Passive submission—
the dog rolls on his side
with his hindlegs in the
air and frequently
urinates.

As this Husky meets a man in a Husky suit, he shows his reluctance and surprise by backing off with his tail down.

Signs of dominance are:
    1. Makes eye contact.
    2. Stands with ears up,
tail up and the hair raised
on his neck.
    3. Shows dominance over another dog by standing at
right angles over it.
Dominant dogs tend to behave in characteristic ways
    such as:
    1. The dog may be unwilling to move from his place
(i.e., reluctant to give up the sofa if the owner wants
to sit there).
    2. He may not part with toys or objects in his mouth
and may show possessiveness with his food bowl.
    3. He may not respond quickly to commands.
    4. He may be disagreeable for grooming and dislikes
to be petted.
    Dogs are popular because of their sociable nature.
Those that have contact with humans during the first 12
weeks of life regard them as a member of their own
species—their pack. All dogs have the potential for both
dominant and submissive behavior. Only through
experience and training do they learn to whom it is
appropriate to show which behavior. Not all dogs are
concerned with dominance but owners need to be aware
of that potential. It is wise for the owner to establish his
dominance early on.

A human can express dominance or submission toward a dog in the following ways:

1. Meeting the dog's gaze signals dominance. Averting the gaze signals submission. If the dog growls or threatens, averting the gaze is the first avoiding action to take—it may prevent attack. It is important to establish eye contact in the puppy. The older dog that has not been exposed to eye contact may see it as a threat and will not be willing to submit.

2. Being taller than the dog signals dominance; being lower signals submission. This is why, when attempting to make friends with a strange dog or catch the runaway, one should kneel down to his level. Some owners see their dogs become dominant when allowed on the furniture or on the bed. Then he is at the owner's level.

3. An owner can gain dominance by ignoring all the

Digging is a natural dog behavior and is more effectively channeled than eliminated. Give your dogs a place in the yard where digging is allowed.

You can tell that Mika, Katie and Nessa know Jean Edwards is Top Dog by the way they're obediently sitting by her and posing for the picture.

dog's social initiatives. The owner pays attention to the dog only when he obeys a command.

No dog should be allowed to achieve dominant status over any adult or child. Ways of preventing are as follows:

1. Handle the puppy gently, especially during the three- to four-month period.
2. Let the children and adults handfeed him and teach him to take food without lunging or grabbing.
3. Do not allow him to chase children or joggers.
4. Do not allow him to jump on people or mount their legs. Even females may be inclined to mount. It is not only a male habit.
5. Do not allow him to growl for any reason.

6. Don't participate in wrestling or tug-of-war games.
7. Don't physically punish puppies for aggressive behavior. Restrain him from repeating the infraction and teach an alternative behavior. Dogs should earn everything they receive from their owners. This would include sitting to receive petting or treats, sitting before going out the door and sitting to receive the collar and leash. These types of exercises reinforce the owner's dominance.

Young children should never be left alone with a dog. It is important that children learn some basic obedience commands so they have some control over the dog. They will gain the respect of their dog.

PROBLEMS

Barking

Dogs left tied up in back yards often resort to barking out of loneliness and frustration. Only keep your dog out this way for short periods of time.

This is a habit that shouldn't be encouraged. Over the years I've had new puppy owners call to say that their dog hasn't learned to bark. I assure them they are indeed fortunate but not to worry. Some owners desire their dog to bark so as to be a watchdog. In my experience, most dogs will bark when a stranger comes to the door.

The new puppy frequently barks or whines in the crate in his strange environment and the owner reinforces the puppy's bad behavior by going to him during the night.

If you leave a puppy with something he can chew on, make sure he has your permission, otherwise it's your fault if it gets eaten!

To keep a new puppy from whining or fretting in his crate, give him a chew toy like a Nylafloss® to play with.

This is a no-no. I tell my new owners to smack the top of the crate and say "quiet" in a loud, firm voice. The puppies don't like to hear the loud noise of the crate being banged. If the barking is sleep-interrupting, then the owner should take crate and pup to the bedroom for a few days until the puppy becomes adjusted to his new environment. Otherwise ignore the barking during the night.

Barking can be an inherited problem or a bad habit learned through the environment. It takes dedication to stop the barking. Attention should be paid to the cause of the barking. Does the dog seek attention, does he need to go out, is it feeding time, is it occurring when he is left alone, is it a protective bark, etc.? Presently I have a ten-week-old puppy that is a real loud mouth, which I am sure is an inherited tendency. Both her mother and especially her grandmother are overzealous barkers but fortunately have mellowed with the years. My young puppy is corrected with a firm "no" and gentle shaking and she is responding. When barking presents a problem for you, try to stop it as soon as it begins.

There are electronic collars available that are supposed to curb barking. Personally I have not had experience with them. There are some disadvantages to to the collar. If the dog is barking out of excitement, punishment is not the appropriate treatment. Presumably there is the chance the collar could be activated by other stimuli and thereby punish the dog when it is not barking. Should you decide to use one, then you should seek help from a person with experience with that type of collar. In my opinion I feel the root of the problem needs to be investigated and corrected.

In extreme circumstances (usually when there is a problem with the neighbors), some people have resorted to having their dogs debarked. I

Puppies will pull against the leash and try to jump up on strangers to try to greet a new friend.

caution you that the dog continues to bark but usually only a squeaking sound is heard. Frequently the vocal cords grow back. Probably the biggest concern is that the dog can be left with scar tissue which can narrow the opening to the trachea.

Jumping Up

Personally, I am not thrilled when other dogs jump on me but I have hurt feelings if they don't! I do encourage my own dogs to jump on me, on command. Some do and some don't. In my opinion, a dog that jumps up is a happy dog. Nevertheless few guests appreciate dogs jumping on them. Clothes get footprinted and/or snagged.

I am a believer in allowing the puppy to jump up during his first few weeks. In my opinion if you correct him too soon and at the wrong age you may intimidate him. Consequently he could be timid around humans later in his life. However, there will come a time, probably around four months of age, that he needs to know when it is okay to jump and when he is to show off good manners by sitting instead.

Some authorities never allow jumping. If you are irritated by your dog jumping up on you, then you should discourage it from the beginning. A larger breed of dog can cause harm to a senior citizen. Some are quite fragile. It may not take much to cause a topple that could break a hip.

How do you correct the problem? All family members need to participate in teaching the puppy to sit as soon as he starts to jump up. The sit must be practiced every time he starts to jump up. Don't forget to praise him for his good behavior. If an older dog has acquired the habit,

Baby puppies jump up as a natural response to a big person's attention. You don't have to correct this habit until the puppies are older.

grasp his paws and squeeze tightly. Give a firm "No." He'll soon catch on. Remember the entire family must take part. Each time you allow him to jump up you go back a step in training.

Biting

All puppies bite and try to chew on your fingers, toes, arms, etc. This is the time to teach them to be gentle and not bite hard. Put your fingers in your puppy's mouth and if he bites too hard then say "easy" and let him know he's hurting you. I

If your puppy starts nipping or biting you, say "No" and immediately offer him a chew toy like a durable Nylabone.®

squeal and act like I have been seriously hurt. If the puppy plays too rough and doesn't respond to your corrections, then he needs "Time Out" in his crate. You should be particularly careful with young children and puppies who still have their deciduous (baby) teeth. Those teeth are like needles and can

These older puppies are play wrestling and biting and won't hurt each other.

leave little scars on youngsters. My adult daughter still has a small scar on her face from when she teased an eight-week-old puppy as an eight-year-old.

Biting in the more mature dog is something that should be prevented at all costs. Should it occur I would quickly let him know in no uncertain terms that biting will not be tolerated. When biting is directed toward another dog (dog fight), don't get in the middle of it. On more than one occasion I have had to separate a couple of my dogs and usually was in the middle of that one last lunge by the offender. Some authorities recommend breaking up a fight by elevating the hind legs. This would only be possible if there was a person for each dog. Obviously it would be hard to fight with the hind legs off the ground. A dog bite is serious and should be given attention. Wash the bite with soap and water and contact your doctor. It is important to know the status of the offender's rabies vaccination.

Digging

Bored dogs release their frustrations through mischievous behavior such as digging. For the life of me I do not understand why people own dogs only to keep them outside. Dogs shouldn't be left unattended outside, even if they are in a fenced-in yard. Usually the dog is sent to "jail" (the backyard) because the owner can't tolerate him in the house. The culprit feels socially deprived and needs to be included in the owner's life. The owner has neglected the dog's training. The dog has not developed into the companion we

When a dog has been trained to do basic commands like "Stand," you have more control over him and can ask him to behave.

Siberian Huskies have minds of their own, and though loyal, will go off and explore on their own if you don't supervise them.

desire. If you are one of these owners, then perhaps it is possible for you to change. Give him another chance. Some owners object to their dog's unkempt coat and doggy odor. See that he is groomed on a regular schedule and look into some training classes.

Submissive Urination

This is not a housebreaking problem. It can occur in all breeds and may be more prevalent in some breeds. Usually it occurs in puppies but occasionally it occurs in older dogs and may be in response to physical praise. Try verbal praise or ignoring your dog until after he has had a chance to relieve himself. Scolding will only make the problem worse. Many dogs outgrow this problem.

The Runaway

There is little excuse for a dog to run away since dogs should never be off leash except when supervised in the fenced-in yard.

I receive phone calls on a regular basis from prospective owners that want to purchase a female since a male is inclined to roam. It is true that an intact male is inclined to roam, which is one of the reasons a male should be neutered. However, females will roam also, especially if they are in heat. Regardless, these dogs should never be given this opportunity. A few years ago one of our clients elected euthanasia for her elderly dog that radiographically appeared to have an intestinal blockage. The veterinarian suggested it might be a corncob. She assured him that was not possible since they hadn't had any. Apparently he roamed and

To prevent your dog from making a quick escape, have his leash and collar ready to put on him when you take him out of his crate.

raided the neighbor's garbage and you guessed it—he had a corncob blocking his intestines. Another dog raided the neighbor's garbage and died from toxins from the garbage.

To give the benefit of the doubt, perhaps your dog escapes or perhaps you are playing with your dog in the yard and he refuses to come when called. You now have a runaway. I have had this happen on a smaller scale in the house and have, even to my embarrassment, witnessed this in the obedience ring. Help! The first thing to remember is when you finally do catch your naughty dog, you must not discipline him. The reasoning behind this is that it is quite possible there could be a repeat performance, and it would be nice if the next time he would respond to your sweet command.

Dogs want to guard what think is theirs, from food to toys to your bed. Don't let this instinct get out of control.

Always kneel down when trying to catch the runaway. Dogs are afraid of people standing over them. Also it would be helpful to have a treat or a favorite toy to help entice him to your side. After that initial runaway experience, start practicing the recall with your dog. You can let him drag a long line (clothesline) and randomly call him and then reel him in. Let him touch you first. Reaching for the dog can frighten him. Each time he comes you reward him with a treat and eventually he should get the idea that this is a nice experience. The long line prevents him from really getting out of hand. My dogs tend to come promptly within about 3 to 4 feet (out of reach) and then turn tail and run. It's "catch me if you can." At least with the long line you can step on it and stop him.

Food Guarding

If you see signs of your puppy guarding his food, then you should take immediate steps to correct the problem. It is not fair to your puppy to feed him in a busy environment where children or other pets may interfere with his eating. This can be the cause of food guarding. I always recommend that my puppies be fed in their crates where they do not feel threatened. Another advantage of this is that the puppy gets down to the business of eating and doesn't fool around. Perhaps you have seen possessiveness over the food bowl or his toys. Start by feeding him out of your hand and teach him that it is okay for you to remove his food bowl or toy and that you most assuredly will return it to him. If your dog is truly a bad actor and intimidates you, try keeping him on leash and perhaps sit next to him making happy talk. At feeding time make him work for his reward (his dinner) by doing some obedience command such as sit or down. Before your problem gets out of control you should get professional help. If he is out of control over toys, perhaps you should dispose of them or at least put them away when young children are around.

Puppies who get all worked up may get rough. It's your job to correct them if they hurt you.

Mischief and Misbehavior

All puppies and even some adult dogs will get into mischief at some time in their lives. You should start by "puppy proofing" your house. Even so it is impossible to have a sterile environment. For instance, if you would be down to four walls and a floor your dog could still chew a hole in the wall. What do you do? Remember puppies

The Brazilian International Champion Innisfree's Molly Maguire doesn't suffer from separation anxiety, she's usually with her handler. should never be left unsupervised so let us go on to the trusted adult dog that has misbehaved. His behavior may be an attention getter. Dogs, and even children, are known to do mischief even though they know they will be punished. Your puppy/ dog will benefit from more attention and new direction. He may benefit from a training class or by reinforcing the obedience he has already learned. How about a daily walk? That could be a good outlet for your dog, time together and exercise for both of you.

Separation Anxiety

This occurs when dogs feel distress or apprehension when separated from their owners. One of the mistakes owners make is to set their dogs up for their departure. Some authorities recommend paying little attention to the pet for at least ten minutes before leaving and for the first ten minutes after you arrive home. The dog isn't cued to the fact you are leaving and if you keep it lowkey they learn to accept it as a normal everyday occurrence. Those dogs that are used to being crated usually accept your departure. Dogs that are anxious may have a serious problem and wreak havoc on the house within a few minutes after your departure. You can try to acclimate your dog to the separation by leaving for just a few minutes at a time, returning and rewarding him with a treat. Don't get too carried away. Plan on this process taking a long time. A behaviorist can set down a schedule for you. Those dogs that are insecure, such as ones obtained from a humane shelter or those that have changed homes, present more of a problem.

Remember dogs are dogs and will behave as such even though we might like them to be perfect little people. You and your dog will become neurotic if you worry about every little indiscretion. When there is reason for concern—don't waste time. Seek guidance. Dogs are meant to be loved and enjoyed.

Train your dog to accept your absence by only leaving him briefly at first and gradually increasing the time you're away from him.

SUGGESTED READING

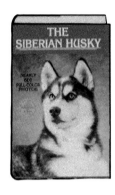

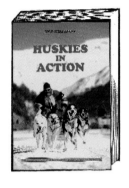

TS-205
Successful Dog Training
160 pages, over 130 full-color photos.

TS-148
The Siberian Husky
512 pages, over 600 full-color photos.

TS-234
Huskies in Action
140 pages, over 120 full-color photos.

TS-249
Skin & Coat Care for your Dog
224 pages, over 190 full-color photos.

TS-214
Owner's Guide to Dog Health
432 pages, over 300 full-color photos.

TS-252
Dog Behavior and Training
288 pages, nearly 200 full-color photos.

INDEX